Pictorial History
of the
Machine Gun

The frontispiece shows Lt J. C. Barrett, 1/5th Bn Leicestershire Regiment, winning his V.C. at Pontruet, September 24, 1918.

From the original painting by Terence Cuneo.

Major F. W. A. Hobart (Retd)

PICTORIAL HISTORY
OF THE
MACHINE GUN

Drake Publishers Inc
NEW YORK

Published in 1972 by Drake Publishers Inc
381 Park Avenue South
New York, N.Y. 10016

ISBN 87749–216–6

*To Barbara, without whose encouragement
I would never have finished this book*

© F. W. A. Hobart, 1972

Printed in Great Britain

Contents

Foreword

by LIEUTENANT-GENERAL SIR NAPIER CROOKENDEN,
KCB, DSO, OBE

THE MACHINE GUN ranks with Gun Powder, the Tank and Nuclear Energy, as one of the major influences on the use of force by the nations and peoples of the world and has therefore played a major part in shaping the destiny of mankind. This book will clearly be of great interest to many people with widely differing views on the management of violence and it will certainly be of value to all those who follow the profession of Arms. For the student of Applied Thermodynamics, for Designers and Inventors, it will serve as an invaluable work of reference, as a source of technical examples, as a reminder of the pitfalls awaiting Designers and as a warning to Inventors of the difficulties awaiting them in securing the necessary support for their projects from Governments and from Industry.

However much one may deplore the use of force, it must be admitted that men who are trained to become expert in the use of a reliable and effective Machine Gun and have used it in war, develop a real affection for it. This is clearly shown in the case of the Vickers gun used by the British Army from 1912 to 1960 and in the remarkable esprit de corps developed first in World War I by the Machine Gun Corps and continued in World War II in the Machine Gun Companies and Battalions of our Infantry regiments. Thousands of British soldiers will remember the relief and reassurance produced in battle by the steady tapping sound of our Vickers gun firing in support, on the flanks or overhead. And will remember, too, the hollow feeling in the stomach on hearing for the first time—or in the wrong direction—the rapid rattle of the German MG 42.

There is no doubt that the Machine Gun has been a major influence on the fate of our own and future generations. This book makes a real contribution to the study of this influence and fills effectively a serious gap in the available literature.

Introduction

THE MACHINE GUN has had an abrupt and terrible impact on the lives of everyone in the 20th Century. From the invention of Maxim's 'First' Model in 1883 the entire pattern of war has changed. The deadly effect of the devastating fire of machine guns was directly responsible for the trench warfare of 1915–18. Together with barbed wire it made the defence supreme. From this situation emerged the tank—which was initially only a mobile, protected machine-gun carrier—and a further change in the conduct of mobile operations.

The addition of the machine gun to the airplane turned it from a reconnaissance vehicle into a fighting machine capable of defending itself in the execution of its mission. From this came the fighter aircraft and the aerial battles of two World Wars.

The casualty lists of World War I were a direct reflection of the effectiveness of the Machine Gun and the loss of the finest young men in Europe during that war has had a profound, far reaching effect on the subsequent events of the last half century. The results of the development of the Machine Gun make worthwhile the study of its origin and progress to date.

"Machine Guns" are generally taken to cover weapons producing an automatic cycle of continuous fire without the aid of external agencies such as hand cranks—or electric motors—from rifle calibres up to and including 30 mm guns, but in a book of this size I have had to limit myself, with a few exceptions, to weapons not exceeding .5 inch (12.7 mm) calibre. I have tried to combine the interests of the expert who desires to see all the variations of each model, with those more concerned with the experimental and unusual weapons.

I hope I have succeeded.

F.W.A.H.

9

Acknowledgements

I have to acknowledge my debt to Lt Col G. M. Chinn USMCR, whose book *The Machine Gun* is the most comprehensive and detailed reference that I know. I have drawn heavily on its contents.

The u/m reference books have all been consulted in the quest for information.

Book of the Machine Gun by Major F. V. Longstaff and A. Hilliard Atteridge. 1917.

The Gatling Gun by Paul Wahl and Don Toppel. 1965.

History of Modern US Military Small Arms Ammunition, Vol I, by F. W. Hackley, W. H. Woodin, and E. L. Scranton. 1967.

International Armament, Vol II, by G. B. Johnson and H. B. Lockhoven. 1965.

Machine Guns (incorporating the Official History of the Machine Gun Corps) by Lt Col G. S. Hutchinson, DSO. 1938.

Machine Guns of the United States, 1895–1946 by Major B. R. Lewis. 1945.

My Life by Hiram S. Maxim.

Superiority of Fire by Major C. H. B. Pridham. 1945.

Text Book of Small Arms. 1929. HMSO.

Vickers—A History by J. D. Scott.

In addition to the above, the Proceedings of:

    The Ordnance Board
    The Royal Artillery Institution
    The Royal United Services Institution
    The Small Arms Committee

have been invaluable.

Of the many people who have assisted me I wish in particular to express my gratitude to the Commandant, the Royal Military College of Science for permission to photograph weapons held there and to the Pattern Room Committee of the Directorate of Inspection of Armaments who allowed me to photograph the magnificent collection of Small Arms held in the Pattern Room at the Royal Small Arms Factory, Enfield.

I am grateful to the staff of the Photographic Library of the Imperial War Museum and Mr Reid, Director of the Army Museum and one time Assistant Keeper of the Tower of London, for their help.

Lastly, I would like to thank Mr Woodend of the Pattern Room, RSAF, Enfield, who went far out of his way to help me.

CHAPTER ONE

Early Firearms

The first gun

THE DISCOVERY of gunpowder and the development of means to use its power to throw a projectile ushered in a new era in warfare. The origin of gunpowder is unknown. The Chinese are credited with its invention and the Gentoo Legal Code written about 1400 BC contains an admonition which has been translated as "The Magistrate shall not make war with a poisonous weapon or with cannons, guns nor yet any kind of firearm". This of course like many translations from old documents is of dubious value because the terms used are open to several interpretations and may have in fact referred to boiling lead or similar concoctions poured from the walls of fortified buildings to repel attacks. They could even refer to "Greek fire".

Professor J. R. Partington, Emeritus Professor of Chemistry at London University in his book *A History of Greek Fire and Gunpowder* concludes that the Chinese did not have gunpowder. He also shows that contrary to popular belief Roger Bacon did not discover it. Roger Bacon (1219–92) was a chemist whose experiments led him into trouble with the Church. It was alleged that he mixed powder in a mortar and there was a great explosion with flame and light and the Devil appeared to do his bidding. To defend himself against the charge of practising the black arts Bacon published a paper in 1252 called *Concerning the marvellous Power of Art and Nature and Concerning the Nullity of Magic*.* In this he described a mixture of "seven parts of saltpeter, five of young hazelwood (ie charcoal) and five of sulphur" from which he could produce an artificial fire and the sound of thunder in the air.

Bacon also suggested that an enemy might be blown up bodily or put to flight in terror, but he made no mention of using his mixture to propel a missile. Professor Partington concludes that Bacon obtained his information from Arabic sources. The other popular contender for the distinction of originating gunpowder, the German monk Barthold Schwarze or Black Barthold, he considers is a legendary figure conjured up by the mystic nature ascribed in this period to chemical experiment.

The first practical use of gunpowder was at the Battle of Crecy,

Epistolae de Secretis Operibus Artis et Naturae et de Nullitate Magiae

11

August 26, 1346 when 10 000 English archers and men at arms slaughtered half of King Phillip VI of Valois' army of 40 000 men with a loss to themselves of some 50 soldiers. Although this was a triumph for the longbow, Edward III also used crude cannon firing a 2lb stone ball. These were largely employed on the flanks and were called "stampede cannon" from their primary role of terrifying the enemy cavalry horses.

By 1453 Mohammed II had a battery of cannon of 30in calibre firing a 1 200lb stone. Some 60 oxen were required to pull each gun which when in action fired at the rapid rate of seven rounds a day.

The first hand held weapons were small cannons fitted with a wooden stave that the firer placed under his arm. They were muzzle loaded. The powder was poured in, a wad pushed down over it and then the ball dropped in. Often another wad was put in if time allowed, to stop the ball rolling out. Ignition of the powder was by means of a slow-match burning at about 2in an hour, which the gunner applied to the primed touch hole. This was called a cannon lock where "lock" means "method of ignition". Later this match was held in an S shaped piece of metal—the serpentine—with the other end forming the "trikker".

After the 16th century came the wheel-lock in which a spring loaded wheel with a knurled periphery was released by the trigger to rotate against a piece of flint, so producing a shower of sparks into the primed flash pan. The principle survives in the modern cigarette lighter. This method was expensive and could not easily be repaired by village craftsmen so a simpler, cheaper, more robust method was developed. This was the flint lock. The knapped flint was held in a cock—or jaws—and when the trigger was operated a spring rotated the flint into contact with a steel plate placed over the priming pan to keep the powder dry. The plate was pushed forward, the spark from the contact flew into the powder and the flame passed through the touch hole to ignite the main charge. This system remained in use right up to the Crimean War. In fact flint lock guns were made in Belgium for the African trade well after the Great War.

The First Rapid-Fire Guns
Once the hand gun became established ideas began to evolve for methods of producing a larger volume of fire. As early as 1339 the "ribauld" was known. This was a multi barrelled device made up of several iron cylinders, arranged on a cart, with the touch holes adjacent to each other so that they could be fired more or less simultaneously to breach the armoured phalanx of pikemen who protected the bowmen. This method of disposing the tubes led to an obvious analogy and they were known later as "organ" guns. By the time of Louis XII (1498–1515) there were in existence guns with 50 barrels that could be fired together.

It should be noted that all these weapons produced a large volume
of fire delivered over a very short period of time. The idea of producing
continuous fire came later. One of the more interesting ways of achiev-
ing the firing of successive rounds was Puckle's gun in 1718. It must
be clearly understood that Puckle's gun was not a machine gun as we
understand the term. It was a revolver-type weapon with the cylinder
rotated by hand. James Puckle was born during the reign of Charles II
and died in 1724. He was a notary public—what we would call a
solicitor today. He produced a gun which he called "A defence". The
opening lines on the specification of his patent, No 418 of July 25, 1718,
are: "A Defence. Defending King George your country and laws, Is
Defending your selves and Protestant Cause". His gun is now in the
Tower of London. It is mounted on a tripod and would appear to have
been designed for ship board use or possibly as a wall gun. There is a
single barrel and a chambered revolving cylinder behind it. Each
chamber has a flintlock attachment. The gunner brought the cylinder
round by hand and lined it up with the barrel. A half turn of the handle
behind the cylinder screwed the whole cylinder forward and the
tapered end of the chamber entered the barrel and made a gas tight
seal. This idea was much in advance of its time and solved the gas loss
problem that plagues even modern pistol revolvers.

It was reported in the *London Journal* of March 31, 1722 that Mr
Puckle's machine was discharged in the Artillery Fields 63 times in
seven minutes by one man in the rain.

The whole concept was rendered rather implausible by the inventor's
declared intention of firing round bullets against Christians and square
ones against Turks—all through one barrel.

The idea came to nothing and people who had invested in Puckle's
Company lost their money.

Later designs adopted the principle of rotating barrels, with each
barrel carrying a priming pan and being discharged when opposite
the cock which was operated in exactly the same way as in a conventional single barrelled flintlock.

The great impediment to all efforts to increase and control the rate
of fire was the flintlock ignition system. In 1807—on April 11, 1807 to
be precise—the Rev. John Forsyth patented his percussion ignition system. It was called Forsyth's Scent Bottle from its shape (*Plate* (9)). The
system was very simple. The bottle contained mercury fulminate and
was rotatable end over end on a hollow spindle which led through the
wall of the barrel into the chamber. When the bottle was rotated so
that it was tipped up, some of the contents dropped down into the
hollow interior of the spindle. When the bottle was turned through a
further 180° a spring loaded firing pin came over the opening in the

spindle. This was struck by the hammer and driven into the detonating compound. The flash continued down the hollow shaft, through the barrel wall and fired the propelling charge. The percussion lock was one of the two most important single steps in the development of guns (the other was the obturating (or rearward gas sealing) brass cartridge case which made breech loading practical), but Forsyth was very shabbily treated by the Government of the day. He refused to sell his patent to Napoleon for £20 000, and although they used his patent they waited 23 years to pay him a paltry £200. Public outcry made the British Government then increase the offer to £1 000 in 1843 but Forsyth did not live to receive it. Forsyth's later design was called a pill-lock. A nipple was placed on the barrel leading through to the powder charge. In the recessed top of this was placed a pill made of mercury fulminate mixture. The descending hammer crushed the pill and the resulting flash initiated the charge.

Forsyth did the majority of his work in the Tower of London and it is commemorated by a plaque erected there.

In 1808 Pauly a Genevan working in Paris produced a paper sandwich enclosing fulminate of mercury which was fired with a needle shaped plunger. English gunsmiths notably Joseph Manton, worked on detonating compounds and in 1818 the copper cap was adopted in England. This enabled most flintlocks to be converted by replacing the cock with a hammer which struck a "top hat" shaped cap placed over a hollow nipple.

In America a sea captain named Shaw produced a pewter cap to fit over the nipple in 1814. He found the pewter melted and sealed off the flash channel, so subsequently he obtained a patent using a copper cap.

The next step was the obvious one of incorporating the primer and the charge in the cartridge. Christian Sharps—who produced most of the buffalo rifles—introduced a self consuming cartridge case in 1852, Colt and Ely collaborated on a paper cartridge and finally in 1857 Smith and Wesson produced the very first commercial rim fired metal cartridge, following the work of Flobert who put a rim on a percussion cap in 1847. The standard .22 round still in use everywhere is only an improvement on this design. Eventually the centre-fire drawn brass cartridge case was produced. An American named Morse is generally credited with this invention in 1858 which—as I have already said— was one of the two most important developments in small arms. Firstly all the elements of the round, ball, propellant and primer were held and protected in the case. The case itself provided a complete obturation ie rearward gas sealing—and so allowed the introduction of breech loading.

CHAPTER TWO

Hand Operated Automatic Guns

THE FIRST working attempt to produce a rapid firing gun was made by a retired Belgian Army Officer in 1857. He made a pyramid of 50 rifle barrels which he could fire in succession in 30sec and the shots were observed to fall two kilometres away.

In England in 1857 Sir James Lillie combined the multi-barrel system with the revolving chamber. He located two rows of barrels, one above the other, each with its own revolving cylinder. Each chamber carried its own percussion nipple. On the right hand end of each row of barrels was a handle and rotation of the handle fired the barrels in turn. The lower row of barrels had cylinders with larger numbers of chambers. The device was never used and is now in the Rotunda museum at Woolwich where the photograph (*11*) was taken.

The American inventors were very much more active than those in Europe and some of their early designs were extremely ingenious. For example a man named C. E. Barnes, residing at Lowell in Massachusetts took out a patent* for a self cocking, percussion fired, crank operated gun. It fired a round with a linen cartridge case. The linen was impregnated to render it combustible and also to stiffen it so that it could be rammed home into the chamber. A tray on the left of the gun held the rounds and there was a toggle joint arrangement to load and lock the breech. The toggle joint was a feature of this gun that showed how far ahead of its time it was. Before the gun could be fired by the continued rotation of the hand crank a percussion cap was mechanically placed over the nipple. When the gun was fired gas pressure bled back through the nipple and pushed back the hammer against the firing spring until it travelled over a sear and was held back in preparation for firing the next shot.

Another machine gun designed to fire paper cartridges was that of Ripley, an American. He never produced a gun but many of his ideas appeared in other guns at a later date. His weapon had nine fixed barrels and a pre-loaded cylinder behind them. A spring loaded firing pin went forward when aligned with the nipple of each barrel in turn as the cylinder rotated. The whole cylinder came off and was replaced with a new one.

* *US Patent 15315 dated July 8, 1856.*

15

The greatest stimulus to weapon design comes in time of war. The American Civil War 1861–65 proved a great boon to inventors of all sorts and machine guns made great strides during this period.

The Ager "Coffee Mill" gun was patented in Great Britain before the Civil War by its inventor. It was so called because it had a hopper feed on top and was crank operated like the coffee grinder of that period. The gun should not be confused with the Sharps carbine, some of which had a coffee grinder in the butt.

A steel cylinder took either loose powder and a .58 ball or alternatively a self consuming paper cartridge. At the rear end of the cylinder was screwed a nipple to take a percussion cap. The hopper was loaded with cartridges and one fell by gravity alone, behind the barrel. The manually operated crank pushed it forward and it was locked in place. After locking, the crank motion released a hammer which hit the cap. The empty cylinder was levered out of the gun and the next round fell into its place. Major George Fosberry, VC, the British inventor of the Webley-Fosberry recoil operated pistol revolver, was sent out from London to witness the firing of the gun. He had had a lot of design and some manufacturing experience in India. He saw this single barrelled gun and laughed at the idea of firing 100 rounds a minute. He—like most of his contemporaries—could not believe that the barrel could withstand the heating effect of "7 500 grains of exploded powder and 7lb of lead in each minute". This fearful conservatism was present everywhere and right throughout the Civil War only 50 Ager guns were purchased.

The Gatling Gun

Richard Joseph Gatling was born in Hartford County in North Carolina in 1818 to parents of British stock. In 1847 he entered medical school at Laporte in Indiana and qualified with a degree in 1848. Throughout his life he was known as "Dr" Gatling but popular belief at the time was that he studied medicine only to learn how to protect his family against the virulent smallpox epidemics that were ravaging the country at that time. There is no evidence that he ever practised as a doctor.

Gatling's father invented a machine for planting cotton and another for thinning it. The son invented a rice planting machine and later adapted this to deal with other grain.

In 1861 he started work on a machine gun designed initially to cover bridges and river crossings. He started where the Ager and Ripley guns had led the way with an Ager type feed and steel container for paper cartridges carrying a nipple at the rear end. Unlike the Ripley design the six barrels were revolved by gears operated by a hand crank and each barrel had a bolt acting as a striker to detonate the cap.

In 1862 the first gun was demonstrated at Indianapolis and amongst the large number of spectators was the Governor of Indiana, the Hon O. P. Morton, who was so impressed that he wrote to the Assistant Secretary of War suggesting official tests be organised. Gatling then got Miles Greenwood, Cincinnati, Ohio, to make six demonstration guns. Unfortunately the guns and the drawings for their manufacture were all destroyed in a fire. Undaunted he continued his work and Messrs McWhinny Ridge and Co, also of Cincinnati made him 12 guns to the patent of November 1862 with six barrels of calibre .58, tapered towards the muzzle. These guns fired a new copper cased rim fire cartridge with an amended bolt head carrying two projections, and the percussion cap and nipple of the first model were eliminated.

This modification made the gun a lot easier to load and improved the ignition. However like all revolvers there was gas wash between the front of the cylinder and the breech face and Gatling tried with very limited success to force his steel cylinders forward against the breech before firing by incorporating a steel cam. This was not successful, produced a lot of friction and undue wear but remained until 1865.

At this time Gatling sold 12 guns each with 1 000 rounds at a price of $1 000 for each to General Benjamin F. Butler in Baltimore. General Butler's name is usually recalled in connection with the despicable way he later treated the ladies of New Orleans. He was a man of considerable perception and he personally directed the employment of these guns during the Northern armies' siege of Petersburg, Virginia. However Gatling had no further success with orders during the Civil War because it was believed in the North that he was sympathetic to the South. His place of birth—North Carolina—was in the South—and his choice of Cincinnati to manufacture his guns was believed to have been made with a view to the Southern rebels crossing the Ohio river and "seizing" his production.

Gatling severed his connection with McWhinny, Ridge and Co in 1864 and went to James Cooper of Frankford, Philadelphia to make his new model. Cooper was renowned for precision built firearms and the new guns in 1865 and 1866 incorporating improvements on the earlier models, were a great success.

The most radical change was to form a chamber in each of the barrels and eliminate altogether the steel container which came from the Ager "Coffee mill". A rimfire copper cartridge case and the Minié bullet were used. The cartridge case gave obturation—ie rearward gas sealing—and the Minié bullet expanded outwards to prevent gas leakage past the bullet. The system of loading is shown (*Plate* (*15*)). A helical cam drove each bolt forward in turn when it rotated to the lower right hand position, to chamber a round and lock the breach opening.

As the bolt went forward the spring loaded striker was held up until locking was completed and it was then released to fire the round. The cam gave a period of dwell to cope with hangfires and then the bolt was unlocked and as it was withdrawn an extractor on the bolt pulled the empty case clear of the chamber.

This new gun was tested in January 1865 and hailed by the American Army Ordnance Department with enthusiasm. It was suggested that guns of 1in calibre firing either a lead ball for long range work or a buckshot load for close firing, should be made for trials. These trials were successful and on August 24, 1866 the Gatling gun was officially adopted by the US Army with an order for 50 guns of 1in calibre and 50 of .5 calibre to take the new rounds developed by Colonel Benét of Frankford Arsenal. Gatling converted from .58 to .5 and entered into agreement with Colt's Patent Fire Arms Co to make these 100 guns at Hartford in Connecticut. Colt continued this association for many years.

The end of the American Civil War enabled Colt to start selling the Gatling gun all over the world. A new 10 barrelled version was produced both in 1in and .5 calibre and many European countries were interested in this gun.

At this time the British Army had the Boxer cartridge. This was not a solid drawn brass case but a rolled brass type attached to an iron base. There is no doubt at all that this method of fabrication was inferior to the American type of round but all the same the British requirement was for a Gatling gun chambered to take the Boxer cartridge of 1866. The early trials were invariably terminated by the empty case jamming in the chamber and the extractor tearing through the rim.

Eventually some sort of satisfactory cartridge was produced and the British forces took the Gatling. The Navy were the first to use the gun and later it was adopted for the Army. It still had ammunition troubles as the famous lines of Sir Henry Newbolt recall* but it was used with success against Peru in 1877, the Zulus in 1879 and in Alexandria in 1882 under Captain Fisher who commanded the Naval Brigade.

Undoubtedly the most impressive performance given by the Gatling gun was at the Battle of Tel-el-Kebir in the Anglo-Egyptian war of 1882 where the Naval Detachment of six Gatlings manned by 30 sailors was very effective. This can be judged by the casualty figures— British 39 killed 379 wounded. Egyptian 2 000 killed, 500 wounded and captured.

The Russians bought the Gatling in 1871. They sent General Gorloff to supervise the manufacture and delivery of 400 guns chambered for

* *The sand of the desert is sodden red, | Red with the wreck of a square that broke, | The gatling's jammed and the colonel dead, | And the regiment blind with the dust and smoke, ... From Vitai Lampada*

the Russian cartridge. His name was stamped on every gun and when later the gun was manufactured in Russia it was called the Gorloff.

The Prussian army tried the Gatling in 1869. Their infantry at this time had the Dreyse Needle Gun and a comparative firing was carried out at Carlsbad between 100 selected riflemen and one Gatling firing exactly the same quantity of ammunition at targets at 800 metres. The rifles produced 27 per cent hits, the Gatling 88 per cent.

Throughout the world the Gatling was bought or made under license. It played its part in the British process of Christianizing the uncivilised world.

In 1871 the Gatling was modified for a centre fire cartridge of .45 calibre. This was the standard Army calibre and allowed a common round for the rifle and the Gatling gun. The new Gatling was known as the Camel gun because it was designed to be carried on camels, mules or horses. It had 10 barrels and weighed 125lb. General Custer had four of these guns with him—each capable of firing at almost 1 000 rounds a minute—when he set out with his column in 1876 to subjugate the Sioux. He left the Gatlings out of battle with his rear HQ and went forward himself with the cavalry. They were armed with single shot Springfields and with these' they trotted into Geronimo's ambush at Little Big Horn, manned by Indians with Winchester repeating rifles bought from traders. Custer and his command were virtually annihilated—and the Gatlings which could so easily have won the day remained behind in store.

The Gatling was later improved in 1883 when James Accles of his firm patented a drum feed device. This fitted to the gun brought its rate of fire up to 1 200 rounds a minute and increased its reliability.

In 1893 Gatling produced a gun chambered for the .30–40 Krag-Jorgenson rifle cartridge (which was then being adopted as the USA rifle) with an electric motor to revolve the barrels and produce 3 000 rounds a minute. There was a handcrank which could be used if there was no power.

This idea of an electrically powered rotating barrel gun was perfected in the 1960s with the advent of the General Electric Company of America's Vulcan M61 20mm gun and the Mini gun. These will be discussed in a later chapter.

The very last Gatling came out in 1895. It had no handcrank and no electric motor. The barrels were rotated by gas pressure, from a tapping near the muzzle, forcing down a lever which when returned by the force of its spring indexed the barrels round one station.

The Gatling was produced and modified to take the .30–06 round until 1911 when, after active service since 1862, it was declared obsolete. Dr Gatling died in 1903, having developed his gun from loose powder charges through linen, copper, rimfire, centre fire cartridges and hand, electric and automatic operation. He was a great inventor.

The Mitrailleuse

In October 1863 Gatling wrote to Major Maldon of the French Artillery pointing out that a multi-barrel quick firing gun would be more efficient than a gun firing grapeshot or a multi barrel volley type of gun. The French appeared to be interested but the matter was not pursued further because the American Union Government forbade all sales of armaments abroad.

In Europe it was considered that better results came from the simultaneous firing of a large number of barrels which could be readily reloaded. These were called *mitrailleuse* meaning grapeshot shooter. The first such weapon in Europe was designed by a Belgian Army Captain named Fafschamps. He produced some drawings and a very roughly finished prototype which he sold to a well known Belgian engineer called Joseph Montigny who had a factory at Fontaine l'Eveque. Montigny improved on Fafschamps gun, re-named it the Montigny mitrailleuse and persuaded Napoleon III to adopt it for the French army. As we shall see, this was one of the worst day's work that Napoleon ever did. The well known Commandant de Raffye was ordered to build the Montigny mitrailleuse at the Armament Factory at Meuden but the French authorities insisted that the whole project be treated with great secrecy and no one was allowed access to the Arsenal. The finished guns were moved under tarpaulins with an escort and in short, as might be expected, the press played this up as hard as they could and everyone who knew nothing of the project was completely certain that the French had a secret weapon of terrible destructive capacity. What was the truth?

The original Montigny gun had 37 barrels, contained in a single tube. The ammunition was placed in 37 holes in a steel plate. To load the gun the breech block was screwed back and the plate dropped into grooves on the breech block face. The gunner used his left hand to rotate a crank to push the breech block forward and the 37 bullets entered the 37 barrels with the plate acting as a chamber. The cartridge case neck entered the barrel to produce a gas tight seal. After the plate was fully forward, the last movement of the rotating crank cocked all the firing pins.

The gunner then grasped the firing crank which was on the right hand side of the breech. He could either fire all rounds by a single rapid rotation or he could turn the crank as slowly as required. When all chambers were emptied he returned to the loading crank which he now rotated in the opposite direction to withdraw the block and then lift out the plate with 37 empty cases. The plate was banged down over 37 pins on the trail and the empty cases cleared leaving the plate free to be reloaded. For rapid firing several plates were pre-loaded. About 12 plates could be so fired each minute.

The barrel and breech block were mounted through a shield on a two wheeled carriage of artillery pattern with a conventional trail. It weighed 2 tons with 2 100 rounds in a limber.

De Raffye made some alterations to this design. He decided on only 25 barrels and adopted the Chassepot rifle cartridge—at the suggestion it is believed of Major Fosberry. The shallow Metford rifling was adopted because the lack of sharp edges to the lands made it suitable for the black powder charge.

When war came in 1870 between Prussia and France the French were victims of their own propaganda. The French commanders used it like a field gun instead of an infantry weapon and the Prussians simply destroyed the mitrailleuse as soon as it was brought into action. There were a few occasions in which the mitrailleuse was employed in close support of the French infantry. One of these was at the Battle of Gravelotte on August 18, 1870. The Prussian 38 Infantry Brigade attacked the French position and the concealed mitrailleuse were used at close range with tremendously lethal effect. The French infantry were able to counter attack and a Prussian attempt to use cavalry was a disaster. 72 officers, 2 542 men were killed or wounded. This represented more than 50 per cent of their troops engaged. This was however only a local victory and the main battle was lost. MacMahon was drawn back to Metz. Napoleon and MacMahon engaged the Prussians at Sedan and the Emperor was captured together with 100 000 troops. Most of the mitrailleuse guns were lost at Sedan and the remainder were tied up in Metz with Bazaine's army.

The French later obtained some Gatling guns which were shown by their success in the defence of the crossing of the River Huisne, to be more effective than the mitrailleuse—the secret weapon that wasn't.

The Gardner Gun

William Gardner of Toledo in Ohio was a soldier in the Union Army who worked his way up to the rank of Captain. He had seen various attempts to produce a fast firing gun and devised one of his own. He was unable to get the necessary finance to produce it himself so he sold his patents to a company recently formed in Hartford, Connecticut, Messrs Pratt and Whitney—now one of the great aero engine firms of the world. Pratt had worked for Colt's Patent Fire Arms Co and was an experienced designer.

The gun consisted of two barrels side by side displaced by about

1¼ inches, fixed in a casing—usually of brass—with rear and front barrel rings. The rear ring was extended back to contain the two bolts and behind them an operating crank. The ammunition of .45 calibre, centre fire, was placed in a wooden block with the rims protruding and the whole assembly was pushed down a vertical feed guide above the gun. The rims entered a T slot and the wooden box was pulled forward leaving the ammunition ready for loading. The first round was forced down on to a feed tray between the barrels. This tray had two slots for the passage of the rounds. The tray was swung to one side and a round positioned for ramming. The action of the crank forced the bolt forward and chambered it. When the round was chambered the crank gave it full support and then released the spring loaded firing pin. The crank was so shaped that the full support of the bolt was maintained for about one-fifth of the revolution of the handle so that in the event of delay in the ignition, ie a hang fire, there was no danger. To allow easy extraction of the case a "shell starter" was used which consisted of two crescent shaped pieces that gave a leverage to the case thus providing primary extraction. The crank withdrew the bolt and as it did so the other bolt moved forwards to start the cycle with the other barrel. Each barrel was thus fired alternately as the feed tray swung from side to side. The empty cases were forced out through the bottom of the gun. The top cover was hinged at the front and lifted up from the back after a handscrew had been drawn out.

The gun was very solidly built and the "top dead centre" locking system was very safe.

The weapon was tried on June 17, 1879 at the Washington Navy Yard range and subjected to the most rigorous tests. Amongst other tasks it fired 10 000 rounds in 27min 36sec. This speed of firing for a hand operated gun seems almost incredible but there was no mistake and it had earlier in the day fired 6 631 rounds in 18min 55sec. After this test it was necessary to pour water through the bores to cool them off. Throughout the test there were 5 instances of failure to extract—all on the right hand barrel. During the lunch break the bolt was taken out, the extractor hand filed to remove a burr and bent back a little. It then functioned perfectly.

In spite of all this the American Navy did not buy the gun and the Army appeared to be happy with the Gatling, so Gardner took his gun to England and demonstrated it. The Admiralty laid on a comparative trial with eight other guns. The five barrelled Gardner fired 16 754 rounds, with 24 stoppages, at a rate which at one time was raised to 812 rounds a minute.

It was used in the Sudan in 1884 and was with naval landing parties, mounted on a tripod, in small operations all over the world.

When smokeless powder was invented a belt fed version was produced by an Englishman named Robertson. It was tested but was not successful.

The Lowell Gun

In 1875 the Lowell Manufacturing Co of Lowell, Massachusetts produced a gun (*20, 21*) invented by De Witt Clinton Farrington who formed the company to make his gun. It had four barrels located through two discs. The forward disc was attached to the carriage by trunnions and the rear one locked into the body. When the release catch was operated the rear of the barrel assembly could be swung up and the barrels rotated. The gun fired only through the top barrel and the others were used when the first one got too hot. A barrel change could be effected in seconds, or a jammed case removed.

At the back of the gun was a handcrank which rotated a worm connected to the feed sprocket. Above the gun was a feeder very similar to that described for the Gardner. The ammunition was the .5 calibre 450 gr. ball type developed by Colonel Benét for the Gatling. It was slipped down the T slot and the first round fell into the feed sprocket which rotated it round into line with the bolt. The bolt was driven forward to chamber the round by a cam rotated by the movement of the crank and as it went forward the firing pin was held back until, when the bolt was fully home and supported by the dwell portion of the cam, the pin rode off the cocking plate and was impelled forward by its compressed spring to fire the cap. After firing the bolt was withdrawn. The extractors were unusual in that they were not spring loaded but held the rim in a T slot which was rotated backwards by a cam which released them when the case was clear of the chamber. The empty case dropped on to the second sprocket which rotated it through a hole in the side of the body.

The gun was tested at the Experimental Battery at Annapolis in October 1876. Farrington was so confident of the soundness of both design and manufacture that he asked for two unskilled men to operate the gun during its tests. Two labourers were shown how to fire it and change the barrels round. They fired 2 100 rounds in $8\frac{1}{2}$ min, including a barrel change. That day the labourers fired nearly 10 000 rounds. There was one hangfire which forced the bullet into the barrel but the barrel was changed in 40sec.

After this test some modifications were made to the mechanism and it was tested again in July 1877 at the same place. This time, during a period of $1\frac{1}{2}$ working days the gun fired 50 000 rounds with only two stoppages caused in one case by lack of lubrication and in the other by a hangfire in the extraction sprocket which necessitated hammering the firing pin out of the bolt.

Further trials were conducted later. They all demonstrated the excellence of this weapon but like many other guns of this period it could not be sold because the forces of the new American Union were small and at peace.

The American Navy bought a few, the Russians bought 20, the Californian Prison Service and Cincinnati police bought a few and the Lowell Company went out of business.

The Nordenfelt

This gun was designed by a Swedish engineer named Heldge Palmcranz. He was unable to finance a company to produce his gun and took it to a Swedish banker named Thorsten Nordenfelt who set up a factory in England to manufacture it. He was a very clever salesman and through his English banking connections he was able to ensure that the influential commercial community were aware of his product. The 1880s in England were a period when displays and exhibitions were very much in vogue and Nordenfelt made sure that the gun—now called the Nordenfelt—was on show at every one.

In 1882 he gave a demonstration of a 10 barrelled rifle calibre gun to the Royal Navy at Portsmouth. In this he fired 3 000 rounds in very slightly over 3 minutes. At this time a gun firing 1 000 rounds a minute for any period over a few seconds was very unusual, but the use of 10 barrels each firing 100 rounds a minute makes it easier to understand.

The multi-barrel guns—and they ranged from twin barrels to 12— were all basically the same. The ammunition was placed in a hopper above the breech and was gravity fed through on to a carrier block behind the chambers but not in line with them. The gunner operated a bent lever on the right of the gun backwards and forwards like a pump handle—and as he pushed it forward the carrier block moved to the right so the rounds were lined up with the chambers. The breech block then came forward, chambered the rounds and a toggle joint locked it in position. The last part of the forward movement of the lever moved the action block containing the firing hammers to the right so that the hammers were lined up with the firing pins in the breech block and then released to drive the firing pins into the centre fire cartridges.

When the lever was pulled back the action block was forced to the left, the breech block then moved to the rear extracting the cases, and the carrier block finally came over to the left and was positioned under the hopper to receive the rounds as they were allowed to fall through. The mechanism sounds complicated but it consisted of only the hand lever going backwards and forwards, the carrier block carrying live rounds from left to right, the breech block ramming the live rounds and extracting the empty cases, and the action block which carried the spring loaded hammers from left to right and released each hammer in turn to fire the rounds. A photograph of the breech is included (*23*).

The Nordenfelt guns were made in calibres extending from rifle calibre up to 37mm. They were all manufactured extremely well and were very reliable. The Royal Navy bought the gun in five barrelled versions firing the .45 centre fire cartridge for use in the top of a ship to sweep the enemy decks and the four barrelled one inch calibre for anti-torpedo boat defence.

These guns with five barrels or more had a screw located at the left rear of the breach and this caused the barrels to diverge or concentrate and thus allowed the gun to cover a wider frontage without traversing on the mount.

Surprisingly enough the most advanced and by far the most note-worthy of the Nordenfelt guns was never taken into service. This was a single barrel light machine gun weighing only 13lb. (A modern Bren gun weighs 20lb.) It fired at 180 rounds a minute and required only two men—one to load the hopper and the other to pump the lever back and forwards. The reason for its non-acceptance probably lay with the Machine Gun Committee ruling of 1880 that a machine gun must:— (a) fire 400 rounds a minute (b) have a breech block locked for $\frac{1}{3}$ of a second to prevent damage from a hang fire, and (c) fire 1 000 rounds at a full rate without unduly heating the barrels. These rules were made out at the time when machine guns were multi-barrel affairs and a single barrel machine gun was unknown.

The Nordenfelt Company produced a special rifle calibre armour piercing round which could be fired from this single barrel machine gun—as well as the multi-barrel guns—which had a muzzle velocity of 2 000ft/s and could penetrate 2in of battleship armour at 300yd. It consisted of a hard steel core with a brass or copper envelope to take the rifling. It was well in advance of its time and never came into use.

CHAPTER THREE

Machine Gun Mechanisms

So FAR all the guns described have been hand operated. The rotation of a crank has supplied energy and that energy has been used to carry out a cycle of operations. In every case the cycle has consisted of Chambering, Locking, Firing, Unlocking, Extraction, Ejection, Cocking, Feed.

These stages have not always been in that precise order. For example cocking has sometimes occurred before extraction, but to make any gun work they must all be there. Where the energy has been supplied from outside the gun to provide continuous fire, the gun has been a true "machine" gun. In modern weapons there is very rarely any external source of power and so pedantically speaking they are automatic guns but not "machine" guns. However the expression "machine gun" is so firmly entrenched that it would be pointless not to use it.

The Gun as an Internal Combustion Engine

A gun is basically exactly the same in principle as an internal combustion engine. Chemical energy is fed in, burnt to produce hot gas which expands to drive a piston down the cylinder. In the gun the piston, ie the bullet, leaves the cylinder and does not remain for a repeat of the cycle.

The amount of energy fed in is very considerable—about 1 000 calories per gramme of propellant. Only about 30 per cent of it is used to propel the bullet and the rest is used to heat the chamber and bore, to produce recoil of the weapon, or is wasted as muzzle blast. The actual details of the energy distributions are:—

	percent
Useful work done on the bullet, ie bullet kinetic energy	20–30
Work done in rotating the projectile	3.0
Work done against friction	3.0
Recoil energy (whole weapon recoiling, eg a LMG)	0.1
Muzzle blast	40.0
Heat to barrel	30.0

These figures are approximate and vary from model to model. It can be seen that there are two sources of energy available to the designer to be used to produce an automatic cycle. These are recoil and the gas energy wasted at the muzzle. The ways in which these have been used in the past will be mentioned in the coming chapters.

There are three practical methods of operation—each with several sub-divisions—by which an automatic gun can be made to function and produce repetitive fire. These are Blowback, Recoil and Gas operation.

Blowback

If the breech block of the gun is not locked to the barrel or body it will be driven backwards by the gas pressure driving the cartridge case out of the chamber. This is known as "blowback" or sometimes "spent case projection". It is almost universally employed in sub-machine guns using pistol type rounds and there are now several examples of its use in machine guns employing full power cartridges. In these examples it is necessary to prevent the case moving back too rapidly or the internal pressure will burst the case when it loses the support afforded by the chamber and so delay devices are incorporated in the bolt mechanism. The diagram below shows the French General Purpose Machine Gun— the Arme Automatique Model 1952—the AA 52. Here the lever delays the backward movement of the bolt head which supports the cartridge case, whilst transferring energy to the bolt body which is accelerated backwards. When the chamber pressure has dropped to a safe level, the lever has rotated out of the body of the gun and the entire block is blown back with its two parts still separated. They come together just before firing the next round and the lever once again engages in the recess in the gun body. The gun is shown on plate 166.

Recoil

In this system the breech block is invariably locked to the barrel. The backward pressure of the gas drives the breech block rearwards and the barrel moves back with it. You can always distinguish a recoil operated gun because not only does the barrel reciprocate as the gun is fired but you can push it back with your hand since it is not locked to the body.

If the barrel only goes back about half an inch before the bolt is unlocked to travel back on its own to complete the cycle of operations, the gun is described as "short" recoil operated; but if the barrel travels rearwards by an amount exceeding the length of a complete unfired round, it is known as "long" recoil operated. The latter method is rarely employed these days because it produces a very slow rate of fire and has importance only in the 30mm RARDEN cannon which is carried in British armoured personnel carriers as a counter to the threat of enemy vehicles of a similar kind.

In rifle calibre guns there is a lack of recoil energy and the gas pres-

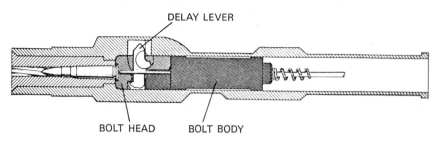

DELAY LEVER

BOLT HEAD   BOLT BODY

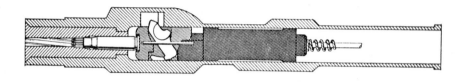

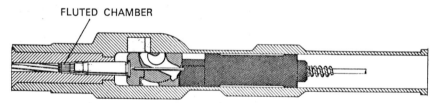

FLUTED CHAMBER

Fig. i. Blowback Operation—The French AA-52.

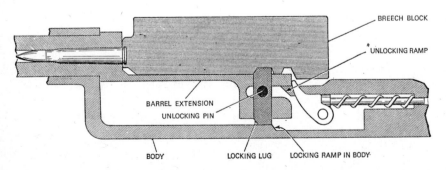

BREECH BLOCK

UNLOCKING RAMP

BARREL EXTENSION

UNLOCKING PIN

BODY   LOCKING LUG   LOCKING RAMP IN BODY

Fig. ii. Short Recoil Operation—The Browning Machine Gun

sure is trapped at the muzzle to drive the barrel back. This is known as "gas assistance" to the recoil operation.

Gas Operation
We have seen that 40 per cent of our energy input is wasted as muzzle blast and some of the gas can be tapped off into a cylinder to drive back a piston connected to the locked bolt. The piston will impart enough energy to the bolt to carry out the complete cycle of operations. This method is very popular because it has the great advantage not possessed by the other two methods, of being adjustable and by increasing the volume of gas through a variable sized port the effects of fouling, sand, mud, etc. can be overcome.

Shown below in diagrammatic form is a typical gas operated gun.

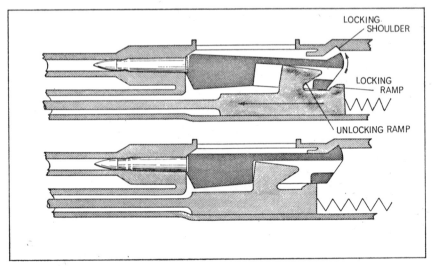

Fig. iii. Gas Operation—The Bren Gun

Locking and Mechanical safety
With the exception of the delayed blow back system all machine guns operate with the bolt locked, either to the barrel or body to ensure the cartridge case is fully supported. The pressure in a modern gun can be up to some 23tonf/in² and the gases in the chamber have a flame temperature of about 2 500K. If the gas was allowed to emerge at this temperature and pressure it would destroy the gun mechanism and inflict grave injuries on the firer whose face is often adjacent to the chamber. To prevent this the design must ensure that until the breech is completely locked the gun cannot be fired and also that until the

pressure has dropped to a safe low level it cannot be unlocked. This is frequently done by ensuring that the firing arrangement operates the locking mechanism before it reaches the cap and building in a period of mechanical delay before unlocking takes place. The actual mechanism for locking the bolt to the barrel or body can take several forms but in machine guns it will generally be a rotating bolt, a tilting block which puts one end into a recess in the body or some form of lug which is forced out from the bolt to enter a recess in the body. Other mechanisms have been used in the past as we shall see when we discuss the Vickers gun, amongst others, in a subsequent chapter.

Feed

The machine gun exists in 3 major categories:— the light machine gun, the medium machine gun and the heavy machine gun. Modern practice is to combine the light and medium machine guns into one, called the General Purpose Machine Gun.

The roles of these guns dictate the type of feed.

The Light Machine Gun is an infantry section weapon, and light weight and the ability to produce immediate fire are important. The feed therefore is from a magazine containing 20–30 rounds which can be quickly removed and replaced by one already filled.

The Medium Machine Gun is a Company or Battalion support weapon and the main requirement is accurate sustained fire. This invariably leads to a belt feed with some 200 rounds in a belt and the ability to join belts to produce continuous fire for a period dependent almost entirely on the cooling arrangement.

The General Purpose Machine Gun is a compromise. It ought to be light enough to be carried in the Infantry Section—but rarely is. It must be sturdy enough to produce sustained fire—which makes it heavy, and in this role it needs belt feed which is not universally acceptable to infantry operating in close country.

The Heavy Machine Gun is a weapon of .5in calibre up to 30mm. It is used as an anti-aircraft gun, anti-armoured personnel carrier gun and in many armoured fighting vehicles. The smaller calibre gun will be belt fed but the great weight of the ammunition in 20mm and 30mm sizes will generally lead to magazines, clips and drums of limited capacity.

Feed Mechanisms

Magazines are easily understood. They contain and protect the ammunition and drive it into the gun, using spring energy. A typical box magazine is shown opposite (Fig. iv).

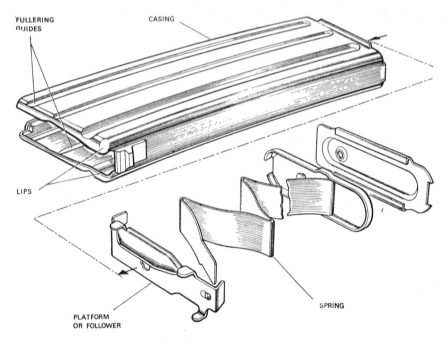

Fig. iv. Box Magazine

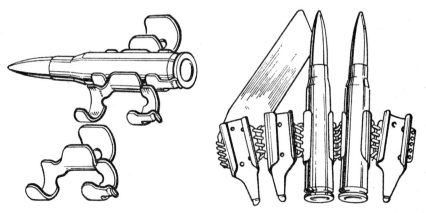

Fig. v. Disintegrating Link Belt   Continuous Link Belt

Belt Feed. The gun must supply the energy to lift the belt of ammunition into the feedway. It is usual to use the reciprocating bolt to supply the energy which will operate a series of pawls pulling the belt through the gun. A stud on the bolt usually runs in a curved path in a feed arm and makes this move across the gun from side to side. The belt is pulled up and held whilst the arm returns, and then pulled up again. A long belt can take a lot of energy out of the system.

Modern belts are of metallic construction and may be in a continuous length or so designed that they disintegrate as they pass through the gun. The continuous belt although it has the disadvantage of hanging out of the gun on the exit side, can be refilled during a lull in the battle. The disintegrating type is more expensive and cannot be reloaded, but it is an advantage to the user not to have a protruding empty belt.

The two types of belt are shown on page 31 (Fig. v).

Extraction and Ejection

With a few major exceptions—such as the Russian medium and general purpose machine guns—all modern machine guns fire rimless—as opposed to rimmed—ammunition. An extractor claw is fitted to the bolt to grip into the cannelure and this will withdraw the empty case from the chamber as the bolt moves back.

The empty case must be cleared from the bolt way to allow the feed stroke as the bolt comes forward again. This is accomplished, generally, in one of two ways. Either the case strikes a fixed projection in the body during the rearward movement of the bolt and this directs it out of

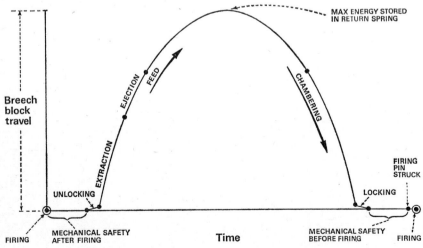

Fig. vi. Automatic Cycle of Operations

the gun or alternatively a plunger comes forward from the bolt face
and drives the case out of the gun as soon as it is clear of the chamber.
The design must ensure that the hot case is projected well clear of the
gun and the gun's crew.

The Automatic Cycle of Operations
The important aspects of each of the elements of the cycle have been
mentioned very briefly but I hope adequately. These eight parts, ie
chambering, locking, firing, unlocking, extraction, ejection, cocking
and feed can be represented graphically (see Fig. vi).

Barrel Heating
Although it is not the purpose of this book to deal with matters of
detailed design a few words on the methods available to remove excess
heat from the machine gun barrel will help to explain the way in which
the weapon has developed.

The modern GPMG will fire at a cyclic rate of about 750–1000
rounds a minute. The energy input from this is approximately 200
horse power. This is equivalent to the output of six Mini cars so we can
picture our input thus:

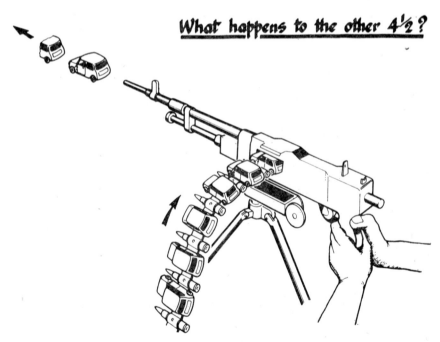

Fig. vii. Energy input into a modern Machine **Gun**

P.H.M.G.—C

The bullets coming out represent about 50hp or $1\frac{1}{2}$ Minis. These are shown emerging from the muzzle. The remaining $4\frac{1}{2}$ Mini's worth of energy has either escaped out of the muzzle with the expanding gases or remained in the gun to heat the chamber, barrel and working parts. This heating effect is the problem.

The structure of the steel is such that it must not be allowed to reach a temperature in excess of 550°C and when it has reached this temperature the gases are transferring 10hp to the barrel, ie seven or eight electric bar fires.

With the bore at 550°C and the outside air at 15°C the outer surface of the barrel is at 525°C and only $2\frac{1}{2}$hp is being lost to the air. The barrel is then taking in 10hp and only losing $2\frac{1}{2}$hp and therefore increasing in temperature, so the problem is simply this. How can more heat be passed from the barrel to the surrounding air?

The best way is to surround the barrel with a water jacket and let the heat boil off the water. This means a gun with about 10lb of water to be carried by the soldier. He must replace the water—even using condenser cans there is a loss—and the steam emerging will give his position away.

If we cannot accept water, then to rely on air cooling means that the barrel must be changed after every 300–400 rounds depending on the rate of fire and how massive the barrel is. The more metal in the barrel the more heat it can absorb before it must be changed.

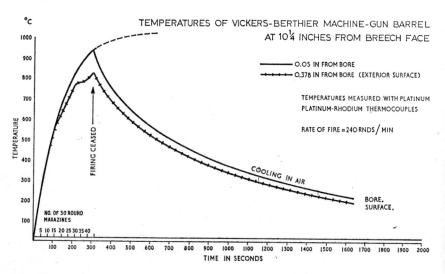

Fig viii. Barrel temperature v no. of rounds fired and time

Finned barrels only help when there is a wind blowing across them and so although the finning is useful in a vehicle mounted gun it is not much help to the infantry and the dirt and oil in the fins burns off to produce a heat haze across the sight line.

The weapons shown in this book reflect the various ways in which the problem has been tackled in the past. The Lowell gun—see (21) —had four barrels which were changed round as they heated up. There are many water cooled barrels shown on various equipments and also changeable air cooled barrels.

Modern thought concentrates on using liners which are not of steel but alloys usually of Stellite, which retain their strength at high temperatures—see page 83—or a "smear" which is put on the interior of the barrel from an additive to the propellant which protects the bore. This solution although suitable in a big gun is difficult to apply to a machine gun where the cartridge is already full of propellant.

No satisfactory solution seems in sight and we can expect to see machine guns using the coolest propellant available and with spare barrels carried by the gun team, for many years to come.

CHAPTER FOUR

Maxim Machine Guns

THE NAME of Maxim stands out head and shoulders above his contemporaries. He was a giant amongst inventors. The range and breadth of his inventive genius is almost beyond belief. In nearly every subject that attracted his attention he invented something that other lesser men had been constrained to dream about. No matter how small or how large the problem, he contributed something new. The variety of his inventions ran from automatic self-setting mouse traps through gas lighting, electric lighting, rifles, silencers, machine guns, cannon and finally a steam driven aeroplane that flew.

Maxim's ancestors were Huguenots who left France to escape religious persecution and settled in Canterbury. They left England, according to Maxim's autobiography *My Life* and went to America where they settled in Massachusetts. There, he said "they could worship God according to the dictates of their own conscience, and prevent others from doing the same". H. C. Maxim was born in Sangersville, Maine, on Feb 5, 1840. He had very little formal education but worked long hours in a variety of tasks. Firstly he was apprenticed to a carriage maker, then made agricultural rakes, and after four years at that sort of work he set up and operated his own grist mill. The mill was overrun with mice and he invented a trap that re-set itself each time it caught a mouse. He made no money on this but the idea was taken up by a manufacturer who made a comfortable income from it. He became tired of working for payment in grain and took up a wood turner's job. He was powerfully built, fond of fighting and was employed as a barman where his physical powers in clearing out awkward customers brought him great respect. The Civil War broke out and Maxim moved to Canada. His business opponents later capitalised on this and accused him of dodging the draft, but since his two elder brothers were already fighting, and it was not the Draft Board's policy to take more than two from one family, this is not a fair accusation. He came back to work for his uncle who was making gas lighting machines. Maxim invented an improved machine which his uncle started to make. Maxim then thought up a better one which infuriated his uncle who had just tooled up so Hiram was sacked. He moved to Boston and invented an automatic sprinkler type fire extinguisher which was the forerunner of those used today in all big stores and warehouses. He then set up, by himself, the

36

Maxim Gas Company, which was successful. He saw the way events were moving and invented an electric light bulb and in 1881 he went to the Electrical Exhibition in Paris. He realised then that the European countries were in such an agitated state that a successful machine gun could bring him a fortune. He completed his electrical work and returned to London where he set up an office and workshop at 57d, Hatton Garden.

He brought with him a milling machine and purchased an American lathe, planer, drill and press. With these he was all set to start inventing.

He first examined those principles of automatic operation which he hoped to employ. He took a Winchester magazine rifle and interposed a sprung plate between the butt and his shoulder. When the rifle fired the spring was compressed and when it re-asserted itself a series of rods operated the under lever and re-charged the magazine. This rifle was never produced commercially but he saw it as vindicating his ideas and proving that the method of recoil operation was completely practical.

Between 1883 and 1885 he patented every method he could conceive of to operate an automatic gun. Many of these have been tried out and most of them have worked. He made a rig which allowed the setting and adjusting of the positions of the various components of the design and which enabled him to analyse the force exerted by the black powder and ascertain for just how long the breech block and barrel must remain locked together.

In 1884 he was ready to demonstrate what is now called his "first" model (25), using the solid drawn brass cartridge of .450 calibre designed for the Martini Henry rifle. This "first" model represented the first successful attempt to use the propellant power to operate an automatic cycle.

The gun did not have elegant lines. It was 4ft 9in from the muzzle to the rear of the firing mechanism casing, and stood $3\frac{1}{2}$ft high on the tripod.

The method of operation was short recoil. The barrel carried a massive hook, mounted between two lugs, which dropped down over a step in the top of the bolt and locked barrel to bolt. After firing, the barrel and bolt recoiled together for $\frac{7}{16}$in until the hook was lifted out of the bolt by passing under a bridge which levered it up. The bolt was then driven back at increased speed by an accelerator which took energy from the barrel and transferred it to the breech block and the crank. The crank was modelled on that used in the Gardner and to avoid the problem of ever increasing the rotational momentum if the crank continued rotating, its movement was restricted to three-quarters of a circle. The gun fired at each end of the crank stroke.

The gun had a rate of fire controller which could be set from about

1 round/minute to the full cyclic rate of about 600 rounds a minute. The setting regulated an hydraulic valve and the wider open the valve the more oil flowed and there was little resistance to the gun running out. If the valve was strangled there was little oil flowing and the run out—and rate of fire—was slow.

The feed of the "First" model was very unusual, consisting of a magazine of twelve chambers located between the teeth of a sprocket wheel. The belt ran over one sprocket and the rounds were picked up by the meshing magazine sprocket and then transported by the bolt movement.

Once he had fired several thousand rounds and was satisfied that the system was both sound and reliable in its functioning Maxim used what would now be called a "press release". He drew attention to his gun and invited inspection. Amongst his earliest visitors was the Duke of Cambridge followed by Lord Wolsely and a mass retinue of the Staff.

In 1884–1885 Maxim decided to simplify his gun, lighten it and improve the feed. He abolished the crank wheel and the hook locking and substituted the now very familiar toggle joint. The "first" model went to the Science Museum—South Kensington. It is now in the US Marine Corps Museum at Quantico, Virginia.

The production Maxim was operated as a short recoil gun. The breech block—or "lock" as it was called—was held up to the breech face by a toggle joint which fired the gun as it moved beyond the straight line position. The recoil force drove the lock rearwards and since the toggle joint was anchored to sideplate extensions of the barrel the barrel came back as well. After a quarter of an inch travel of the barrel and block the gas pressure in the chamber was down to atmospheric. A tail attached to the rear arm of the toggle joint then was forced to roll against a fixed roller on the casing and this forced the joint open and the lock was accelerated backwards. In the Maxim gun as such, the toggle broke downwards. The Vickers pattern guns—of which we shall hear more later—had the toggle moving up to separate the lock from the barrel but were otherwise the same.

The last movement of the toggle arm backwards over the roller levered the side plates and the barrel forward to the run out position. The Maxim gun was the only gun in which the barrel moved back and forward under the control of the rearward moving breech block. This movement of the side plates—or barrel extension—controlled the feed. A bell crank was rotated back and forth as the barrel reciprocated and the arm of the crank therefore moved from left to right and back again. By a system of spring loaded pawls the feed slide first travelled to the right over the belt and then on the return movement pulled the belt up towards the gun. The rounds used in the Maxim were rimmed and so the design had to withdraw the round from the canvas belt which completely enclosed it and then lower the round for ramming it into the chamber. This was done by having a T-shaped extractor which could move up and down the lock face. As it moved up, when the lock closed up to the breech face, it slipped round the rim of the round in the belt. When the lock went back the round was pulled out of the belt. At the limit of rearward travel the extractor was forced down and the live round was carried down into line with the chamber. The forward movement of the lock forced the round into the chamber and the extractor was levered up the lock face, over the loaded round, to pick up the next round. After firing, a further recoil of the lock carried back a new live round on the top of the extractor and an empty case below it. This empty case either fell out of the bottom of the gun as the lock came forward or was wiped off on the outside of the bottom of the chamber as the extractor came up to collect a live round.

This mechanism was complex and the interplay of the various moving parts is not easy to follow—yet Maxim unaided not only thought it all out but made the parts, assembled them and the gun worked!

In 1884 Maxim approached Vickers, the British ship builders and a new Company was formed called the Maxim Company with Albert Vickers as chairman with manufacturing facilities at the steel works at Crayford in Kent.

The business of demonstrating and selling the Maxim gun then got under way. The War Office demanded that the gun must be capable of firing 400 shots in the first minute, 600 shots in 2min and a 1 000 in 4min. The gun was required to weigh less than 100lb.* After he had met this requirement Maxim put together two of his 333 round belts and fired off the 666 rounds in 1min.

After the demonstration the Government bought three guns. From time to time they purchased more and in 1891 a scale of two guns per Battalion was authorised for the Regular Army. Several Volunteer Battalions purchased Maxim's gun at their own expense but the War Office displayed an indifference that, in retrospect, seems incredible.

Demonstrations were given in France, Italy, Austria and Germany. In Austria a lot of trouble was experienced over cartridges. The Austrians placed a total ban on exporting any of their own rounds and yet wanted the gun to be adapted to their cartridge. Maxim made a sketch and managed to obtain a piece of brass which he had tested for its mechanical properties. When he returned to England he got BSA to make up the cartridge which they did but somehow there was an error in the charge weight and to get the gun to function at all it

---

Minutes of the Proceedings of the Royal Artillery Institution Vol XVI 1889

became necessary to lighten the return spring. On July 7, 1888 the Austrian trial commenced with firings at 200 metres, 400, 600, 1 000, 1 200, 1 400 and 1 575 metres. Finally to test reliability 13 500 shots were fired. The mainspring (which had been lightened) failed after 7 281 rounds and a striker broke after 10 233 rounds. The Austrian report was glowing.

In Germany comparative trials were arranged between the Maxim served by one man, the Gatling with a 4-man detachment, the Gardner with two, and the Nordenfelt with a crew of four. The requirement was to fire 333 rounds at a target at 200 metres. The multi-crew gun did this in one minute and Maxim, alone, achieved it in 30 seconds. The Kaiser watched the trial and those that followed and was greatly impressed. "That is the gun" he said "There is no other". The Germans above everyone else in Europe appreciated the potentialities of the machine gun and studied its tactical application.

In his book Maxim describes how the Russians had no idea at all of what was meant by "automatic". They ridiculed the claim to fire 600 rounds a minute. "No one could turn that crank handle backwards and forwards 600 times in a minute". They were flabbergasted when the handle moved of its own volition. After a lot of delay and official slowness the Russians eventually purchased a large number of Maxim guns and set up a plant to manufacture their own.

The first recorded instance of the use of the Maxim in action was in the Matabele war of 1893 and here 50 Rhodesian policemen indifferently trained but armed with 4 Maxims, beat off 5 attacks from some 5 000 tribesmen. Over 3 000 dead were left in front of the police position.

At the Battle of Omdurman the Dervishes charged the Anglo-Egyptian forces. Of their total casualties of 20 000 three-quarters are ascribed to Maxim fire. When Lt Winston Churchill charged with the 21st Lancers it was into a largely demoralised enemy.

In the Boer War 1899–1902, both sides used the Maxim machine gun. The first full scale encounter in which both sides deployed machine guns on a lavish scale was the Russo-Japanese War of 1904. The Russians used the Maxim of .312 calibre made in England and the Japanese had the French Hotchkiss of .253 calibre made in Tokyo. The Military Attaché's accredited to the two armies sent in their reports and emphasized the part played by the machine guns. Colonel Ian Hamilton—later Commander at Gallipoli—described the battle of Mukden where 16 Maxims fired 200 000 rounds of ammunition without mechanical failure and caused great losses amongst the Japanese assault troops.

The War Office paid little attention to these reports from Manchuria and no more to the official despatches from the North West Frontier of India, where the Chitral campaign had proved a triumph for the

Maxim. In the ten years ending in August 1914 the Vickers Company's deliveries of machine guns to the War Office were just under eleven guns a year.*

The Germans though were a lot more far seeing. They developed the Maxim in 7.92mm calibre at the Government factory at Spandau and produced a sturdy gun carried on a sledge mount. When war broke out in 1914 12 500 Maxims had been issued to troops and their total holding was later said to be 50 000 guns.

In the USA very little was done to adopt a new machine gun when the Gatling obviously should have been phased out. A trial was carried out in 1888 but only a few guns were ordered. In 1904 the Maxim gun was adopted as the standard machine gun of the United States Army but again only a few, totalling 282, were taken into use and in 1912 they were placed in reserve service. In 1913 the Vickers (as it was then called) was tested and recommended for adoption.

Four thousand were ordered from Colt's Patent Fire Arms Co and delivery of these started as the USA entered the war in 1917. By September 12, 1918, 12 125 had been made. Seven thousand were sent overseas but the American forces had few of these.

The Vickers Machine Gun in World War I

In 1888 the Maxim Gun Company amalgamated with the Nordenfelt Company. The Nordenfelt works at Erith were turned over to machine gun production. In 1892 Vickers purchased the Maxim Nordenfelt Co and it was there that the Maxim design was changed to produce the Vickers Machine Gun. The toggle joint was re-designed so that to support the round and fire the gun it fell below the horizontal and the floating axis was supported on the floor of the body. The recoil force tended to drive it down so the lock remained absolutely rigid. After $\frac{1}{4}$in of free recoil the tail of the crank rotated about the roller fixed on the right hand side of the breech casing and the toggle joint rose to withdraw the lock and extract the live round from the belt and the empty case from the chamber.

When war came in 1914 there was complete and hopeless confusion. The Royal Small Arms Factory at Enfield Lock continued for the first two years to produce the Maxim gun and during the first eight weeks of war 1 792 Vickers machine guns were ordered from the Vickers, Sons and Maxim (as the Company was now called) works at Erith. On September 22 an order for an additional 50 guns a week for the French Army was placed. At the same time the skilled manpower was leaving to join up. It took a long time to get production organised on a war

Vickers—A History by J. D. Scott

footing. Output was 40 guns a week in January 1916, 321 a week by December 1916 and in November 1918 it had risen to 5 000 machine guns a month.

The Vickers was undoubtedly the most successful medium machine gun in the War. It was used by the Infantry, the Air Force and the Navy. There were never enough.

The Vickers Machine Gun in World War II

After World War I the Americans concentrated on Browning designs. The Germans developed their own guns—as we shall see—and the Russians produced a family of their own but retained Maxim guns in store. Only the British did nothing between the Wars. A new round, the Mk VIII Z, was developed which with a streamlined, boat tailed bullet, enabled the gun to produce harassing fire out to 4 500yds. The gun was used by Infantry, tanks and the Navy. Production was centred on Crayford.

After World War II the shape of the Army changed. The advent of nuclear weapons imposed a demand for mobility above all. The Vickers gun with 7lb of water weighed 40lb. Its tripod weighed 50lb. Its extreme range became unrequired as the 81mm mortar took over its task and eventually, sadly, on June 1, 1945 the British Army took possession of its last Vickers machine gun.

The Vickers Gun in Larger Calibres

In 1885 the Maxim Gun Company developed a 37mm gun, which embodied all the mechanical principles of operation incorporated in the rifle calibre gun, as an anti-torpedo boat weapon. This originally fired at 400 rounds a minute but later was slowed down to 300. The gun was produced at the invitation of the Admiralty but—as is not uncommon —opinions changed between then and the delivery date and only a nominal order was made.

Maxim did a lot of demonstrating to try to sell the gun. Amongst those to whom he exhibited the weapon's extreme accuracy and high degree of armour penetration was the King of Denmark. He asked the cost of the ammunition and when told it was 6s 6d a round he said "That gun would bankrupt my Kingdom in about two hours".

The French bought a number of guns for harbour defence but when war broke out between the Boers and the British they sold a substantial number, with ammunition, to the Boers who used them very effectively against the guns of the Royal Artillery and the Naval Brigade. At Colenso, for example, firing at 1 200 yards range the Boers put 8 guns out of action in quarter of an hour. This demonstrated to the British Government the mobility, speed into action and extreme accuracy of the gun and a further order was placed. The name "pom-pom" came from the African natives' description of the sound of the gun in action.

The largest Vickers gun of this type manufactured was the 2pr which had a crew of 10 and was used for harbour defence in the early days of World War II. Throughout the War the Navy used multiple versions of the .5 machine gun for anti-aircraft defence (93).

Hiram Stevens Maxim died in 1915. He had been knighted in 1901. It seems that few could claim his breadth of vision and his inventive capacity was immense. He was one of the greatest innovating geniuses of all time.

CHAPTER FIVE

Browning Machine Guns

JOHN MOSES BROWNING was born in Ogden, Utah, in 1855. His father Jonathan was a gunsmith of some note and designed and built two rifles of his own. One was a cap and ball rifle with a magazine fed in from the left. As each chamber came opposite the barrel in turn, the action was jacked forward to make a gas-tight seal. This system gave the weapon the ability to fire a number of shots quickly, and it gave the firer the chance of carrying spare loaded magazines. The other rifle was rather like a very long barrelled six chamber revolver.

John Moses was apprenticed to his father and worked for him for 10 years. His own first patent was bought up by Winchester who manufactured it, a single shot rifle, for several years. He went into partnership with his brother Matthew when their father died. Their first venture was to produce 600 rifles to a dropping block design produced by John and to sell all 600 to Winchester, who also bought the manufacturing rights. Next John designed a lever action repeater which he patented and passed over to Winchester on a royalties basis. This was the famous Winchester '86 model. He then designed the Winchester pump action rifle which is still very popular in shooting galleries, the '90 model. This was followed by the '92, '94, '95 and 1906 rifles and the '97 pump action shot gun. Browning had a disagreement with Winchester over his automatic shot gun and went to Europe. All his pistols and automatic shot guns were produced by Fabrique Nationale d'Armes de Guerre (FN) of Liege, Belgium, who still use his patents.

Browning's First Machine Gun
In 1889 Browning started work on a machine gun *(34)*. He was well aware of Maxim's use of the recoil operated system but his early work convinced him that the energy wasted in muzzle blast would provide a more effective and more controllable source of power. He demonstrated the energy available in such a system by putting a 5lb block of steel in front of the muzzle. The block was 4in square with a small hole in the centre aligned with the bore. After the passage of the bullet the expanding muzzle gases blew the plate across the room. He next used this principle by hanging a plate in front of the rifle muzzle so that when the gas pressure tilted it, it pulled the loading lever forward. A spring restored the lever to its original position and re-charged the chamber.

44

A further experiment was conducted with a magazine fed rifle which was the first truly gas operated weapon in the accepted sense. The barrel was tapped close to the muzzle and the gas led to a piston which carried out all the elements of the cycle of operations. The gun continued to fire at about 16 shots a second so long as the trigger was pulled and ammunition was available.

Browning carried out a great deal of work before his first machine gun was ready. This was designed for the low powered .44 Winchester cartridge. The gun was offered to Colt's Patent Fire Arms Co, in a letter written by his brother Matthew dated November 22, 1890. Colt's made a prototype which was tested by the US Navy in 1893. It was, as a result, re-chambered for the current Navy round which was the 6mm Lee for the Naval rifle. Another similar gun was developed to take the .30–40 Krag-Jorgensen round used by the Army.

In 1895 the Colt gun designed by Browning was fired by the US Navy Board in competition with two hand cranked guns made by Pratt and Whitney and Gatling, and two automatic guns made by Maxim and the French Hotchkiss Company. 50 Colts were ordered in 1896 and a further 150 in 1898.

This first Browning designed machine gun is almost invariably referred to as the "potato-digger". This was because the gas piston acted on a swinging arm, which moved down and back to a vertical position. As a result it could not be fired with the gunner lying prone behind it. The 50 guns first ordered were issued to the United States Marines and they were used in the defence of the British, French, German and American legations in Peking during the Boxer Rebellion in China in 1900.

The gun was known as the model 1895. It was sold to several South American countries and trials were conducted by most of the European powers. One of the sales claims made for the gun was that every time the firing mechanism went forward, cool air was pumped into the chamber, but in fact the gun suffered badly from over heating and "cook-off" was common. To prevent this spontaneous ignition of the charge it was considered necessary to clear the chamber after a lengthy burst if it was not intended to fire again immediately.

In December 1898 a joint Army-Navy Board met and decided to commence a standardization of all small arms, and therefore necessarily ammunition, between the two services. The Navy changed all its 6mm guns to take the .30–40 Krag ammunition and called the modified gun the Colt machine gun Mark I Modification I. The gun was again modified to take the .30 '06 Springfield round.

The Army never adopted the '95 model. On June 14, 1895 an Army Board gave its view that the gun was not wanted in Land Service.

When war came in 1917 Colt produced 1 500 of the '95 model which was known in the Navy as the Mark III and in the Army as the Model 1917. It was used only for training.

It is of interest to note that this gun was modified by Carl Swebilius of the Marlin-Rockwell Corporation and the swinging arm was replaced by what is now considered an orthodox gas piston. This change from the slow development of force provided by the pendulum type lever to a direct thrust, produced extraction problems. The block accelerated so rapidly backwards that the extractor tore through the rim of the cartridge case. This was rectified by increasing the piston mass. The Marlin Aircraft Machine Gun model 1917 was used with a synchronising gear and became the first gas operated synchronised gun to be used by any air force. Later this gun became the first American tank gun.

The Model 1917 Machine Gun

In 1900 John Browning applied for a patent for a short recoil operated machine gun. It is noteworthy that, after all his early work and the '95 model gas operated gun, he should choose to start again with this system and acknowledge that Maxim's selection of the recoil system of operation for a medium machine gun had been correct.

Although the patent was granted in 1901 the Army Board was not interested in a machine gun nor would the Army Department make any financial contribution to the development of such a weapon and so Browning concentrated on his work for FN and produced a steady stream of designs for self loading pistols, game rifles and shotguns.

In 1910 Browning returned to his machine gun patent and produced the prototype at Ogden, Utah. It largely conformed to the 1901 patent but ejection was changed from the right hand side to below the gun and a buffer was fitted to speed up the rate of fire and absorb the surplus bolt energy on recoil. The method of firing was also changed. Browning worked on the gun until he was happy that it functioned as well as anyone could expect.

Very briefly the gun operates as follows. The cartridge is fired with the breech block locked to the barrel extension so the block and barrel recoil together. After about $\frac{1}{4}$in of free travel to allow pressure to drop, the lug locking the breech block to the barrel extension is forced down and the breech block is accelerated rearwards whilst the barrel stops. As the block moves back a transporter pulls a live round out of the belt and places it in a T slot machined in the block face. The entry of this live round displaces the empty case held in the slot on the breech face and it falls out of the gun. The block comes forward, chambers the round, is locked to the barrel extension and pushes the barrel forward. Whilst moving forward the round in the chamber is fired. This so called floating firing cushions the shock of discharge and part of the ammunition impulse is used to arrest the forward movement of barrel and block before driving them rearward. One of the simple but very effective devices in the gun is the method of adjusting the cartridge head space (CHS) ie the distance between the breech block face and the seating face of the round in the chamber. This distance is very important. If it is too small the breech block will not close and the arrangements in the design for ensuring mechanical safety will not permit the gun to fire. If it is too large the cartridge case will move back and the neck may be torn off. With the Browning design the barrel can be screwed backwards or forwards by so many "clicks" of a ratchet and thus the CHS adjusted.

When the United States was on the very verge of entering the World War the Army Department made a survey of its machine gun resources. It found it had available: 282 Maxim guns, of the '04 pattern, which had been in reserve service since 1912, 158 Colt Model '95 (Potato Diggers) and 670 Benét-Merciés. These were a Hotchkiss gun which will be discussed in another chapter. In short, with war inevitable, the total American stock in hand came to 1 100 machine guns, all of which were obsolete. As a result something fairly urgent was needed. On February 27, 1917 at Congress Heights just outside Washington DC Browning demonstrated two weapons. One was his Browning Automatic Rifle and the other was his water cooled machine gun. The BAR will be described later. The test was attended by the Press, and Senators, Congressmen and representatives of the various allied countries. The machine gun did well at this demonstration and in May a further test was put on. Firstly the gun fired 20 000 rounds, without stoppage, at a cyclic rate of 600 rounds/min. It then fired a further 20 000 rounds without failure. The Army Board could not, it appears, believe that such a performance could be expected from a production gun, so Browning produced another gun and fired this for 48min and 12sec, at the full cyclic rate of some 600 rounds a minute. After firing 28 920 rounds the gun stopped for lack of ammunition! Browning then gave a demonstration of stripping and assembling a gun completely blindfold!

The gun had been designed with a view to mass production and contracts were placed with Colts for 10 000, Remington for 15 000 and Westinghouse 20 000. Colts had to prepare drawings and gauges for the other plants and succeeded in producing only 600 guns when the Armistice was signed on November 11, 1918. The Westinghouse Co, made a pilot model in 29 days and the first production gun was completed in 63 days. By Armistice Day it was producing 500 guns a day and totalled 30 150. Remington made 12 000.

It should be noted that these impressive figures had very little bearing on the progress of the war and the American troops in Europe were armed largely with French and British weapons. The first recorded use of the gun in action was on September 26, 1918 when four guns were employed firing 13 000 rounds in 5 days which of course is nothing.

A total of 56 608 model 1917 Browning machine guns were made by the end of 1918. After the War the Model 1917 was modified and called the 1917 A1 and this gun continued in use and was the standard medium machine gun in the American Armies in World War II. It was water cooled.

The aircraft machine gun (which was an air cooled gun) was further modified to produce the Cavalry Machine Gun, the 1919 A2, and this became the 1919 A4 and A6 which were used as the standard section machine gun in World War II and Korea. These guns, basically, are the Model 1917 adapted for a quick change barrel system and air cooling. The Model 1919 Browning in .30 calibre has been used in British Armoured Fighting Vehicles since World War II and is only now being replaced by a British designed variant of the FN MAG.

The Browning Automatic Rifle
It would seem from this nomenclature that this gun was out of place in a book on Machine Guns but in this country it would be classified as a light machine gun.

The BAR is a gas operated LMG with a conventional piston set below the barrel. The bullet passes the tapping and gas forces the piston back inside the cylinder. Attached to the piston is a linkage connecting it to the bolt. As the piston goes back the linkage revolves to give the mechanical safety whilst the chamber pressure is high, and then the linkage is drawn out of the body and the piston, linkage and bolt all go rearwards. The empty case is knocked off the bolt face and leaves the gun, travelling to the right front. When the bolt goes forward it feeds a round into the chamber and then stops. The piston continues forward and the linkage is forced upwards to enter the locking shoulder in the top of the body and act as a strut when the force of discharge is transmitted through the block and linkage to the body.

The weapon can fire either single shot or full automatic—ie it has selective fire—and the rate of fire varies with the selected position of the gas port.

John Browning was working on this gun simultaneously with the Model 1917 recoil operated gun. The BAR was presented to the Press, Military Attachés, Army Board and Senators and Congressmen at Congress Heights on February 27, 1917 on the same occasion as the machine gun. The BAR was an utter and complete success. The Press eulogised it to the heavens and the Government accepted it at once. Browning carried on development work at Colts at Hartford and Winchester did the production drawings. Browning had left America for Belgium years before to find a manufacturer for his commercial weapons after his bitter quarrel with Winchester. It needed a world war to get him working with Winchester again. The first BAR was produced in February 1918 by Winchester and by November production was 300 a day. Marlin-Rockwell produced their first gun in June 1918 and reached 200 a day by November. With Colts and one or two smaller producers the daily total in November 1918 was 706 and 52 000 were produced by that date. The gun first saw action with the US 79 Div on September 13, 1918 but the great majority of American troops saw the war out with French and British guns.

Full details of .30 calibre Browning and Colt Commercial guns are given in the table at the end of this Chapter.

The .5 Calibre Machine Gun

As the war progressed in Europe both sides started to use protective armour plate on vehicles, tanks, gun shields and occasionally individuals. The American Field Commander, Gen. Pershing, initiated a demand for a .5in calibre machine gun. The Commandant of the American Army Machine Gun School obtained a French 11mm machine gun with ammunition and sent it to America for evaluation. It was not particularly advanced and the cartridge was lacking in power. Winchester Repeating Arms Co worked with Browning to produce a .5 cartridge with a ball of about 670 grains and a muzzle velocity of 2 700 ft/sec. Winchester's first effort was a rimmed case but Pershing's staff objected to this and called for a rimless round. Browning brought his experimental gun from Colts to Winchester and stayed with them to try to expedite the design.

Browning's first .50 calibre gun was tested on October 15, 1918. On the first firing it managed 877 rounds in bursts at 500 rounds/min. The bullet weighed 707 grains and the maximum velocity reached was 2 200 ft/s, but this was considered to be partially due to the short barrel length of 30.5in which was the longest that Winchester could rifle. The Ordnance Department accepted that a larger barrel and a better round would bring the muzzle velocity up and ordered 10 000 guns from Winchester.

The first tests of the longer barrelled production gun were not encouraging. The gun was difficult to control, its weight with tripod of 160lb made it very unwieldy and the bullet had a poor armour penetration.

At this stage Winchester had a stroke of luck. They received some captured German 12.7mm (.5 calibre) ammunition for the Mauser Infantry anti-tank rifle. This had a MV of 2 700 ft/s with an 800 grain bullet that penetrated 1in of plate at 250yd. Winchester based their work on the German design and eventually produced the round required.

The gun was basically a bigger version of the Model 1917. A rear sear was fitted to prevent cook off in the waiting period, and an oil buffer was installed to take up the excessive recoil energy from the large propellant charge. There was an adjustable valve, regulation of which allowed variation in the rate of fire.

The water cooled gun was preferred for anti-aircraft use and in that role was standardised as the M1921. The 1921 A1 had a larger water jacket put on in 1930. In 1933 an improved production model of 1921 A1 was designated the M2. This had a 45in barrel—although some earlier guns had a 36-in barrel length. The gun may be fed from either side by repositioning parts of the feed mechanism.

The components of the first aircraft gun in .5 calibre were put together on November 12, 1918. It had the same barrel as the water cooled gun but relied on air cooling. It was not adopted until 1923 and was then called the Model 1921 (aircraft). The model 1923 with feed from either side was redesignated the M2 aircraft in 1933. This gun was used on a flexible mount on aircraft throughout World War II. Nearly two million M2 Brownings were manufactured.

After the 1939–45 war the M2 was modified as a fixed aircraft machine gun and the improved version was called AN-M3. It was used in the Korean War in the F86 fighter which was the principal air to ground attack aircraft.

The M2 was adopted for tank use and is employed in the great majority of US armoured fighting vehicles—usually flexibly mounted as a Commander's gun. It is now used as the ranging machine gun on the latest British main battle tank the Chieftain. The trajectory of the .5 round has been matched to that of the 120mm tank gun and so valuable and limited tank gun ammunition is saved by ranging with the .5 machine gun.

U.S. Ordnance and Commercial Weapons Calibre .30 (Colt-Browning Type)

Item	U.S. Ordnance Weapons	Commercial Weapons	Nature of feed	Remarks
(a)	—	Colt Automatic machine Rifle Cal .30 (R 75)	Magazine holding 20 rounds	Air-cooled, gas operated, shoulder controlled weapon. Can fire either single shot or automatic action. Provided with a bipod fitted to gas cylinder. Can be used in LMG role. Manufactured by Colt's Patent Fire Arms Manufacturing Co. to Browning Patents. Commercial equivalent of gun (c) below with certain distinct differences, eg return spring housed in butt instead of in rear of piston and underneath barrel, pistol grip and magazine and ejection opening covers provided, etc. Has a 24in barrel. Weight 20¼lbs. Obsolete.
(b)	Rifle, Automatic Cal .30 Browning M1918	—	Magazine holding 20 rounds	Air-cooled, gas operated, shoulder weapon. Can fire either single shot or automatic action. Gun stamped "Browning Machine Rifle Model of 1918." Weight 16lb. Obsolete.
(c)	Rifle, Automatic Cal .30 Browning M1918 A1	—	Magazine holding 20 rounds	This is a slightly modified M1918 model with a bipod attached to the gas cylinder. No pistol grip. Can be used in LMG role. Sometimes referred to as Browning Automatic Rifle. Now obsolete. Weight 18½lb.

Item	U.S. Ordnance Weapons	Commercial Weapons	Nature of feed	Remarks
(d)	Rifle, Automatic Cal .30 Browning M1918 A2	—	Magazine holding 20 rounds	This is a further modified M1918 model fitted with a bipod, attached to a flash eliminator secured to the muzzle of the barrel, and a stock rest inserted into the butt. Some models are also fitted with a heavier barrel. A cyclic rate of fire change mechanism is incorporated in the trigger guard assembly. Single shot firing can only be obtained by rapid trigger release when the gun is set for slow cyclic rate of fire. No pistol grip. Weight 21lb. Obsolete.
(e)	Rifle, Machine Cal .30 Browning M1922	—	Magazine holding 20 rounds	This is another modified variation of the M1918 model fitted with a finned barrel, a bipod attached thereto, and a stock rest clamped to the butt. No pistol grip. Can be used in LMG role. Can also be used with bipod and stock rest removed, when it is usually referred to as Browning Machine Rifle. Not in general use. Now obsolete. Weight 22lb.
(f)	—	Colt "Monitor" Automatic Machine Rifle Cal .30 (R 80)	Magazine holding 20 rounds	An improved model of the Colt Automatic Machine Rifle Cal .30 (R 75), fitted with an 18in barrel with a muzzle brake compensator, but without any bipod. Weight 16¼lb. In use by U.S. police departments, prison authorities etc as a "Riot" gun.

Item	U.S. Ordnance Weapons	Commercial Weapons	Nature of feed	Remarks
(g)	—	Colt Automatic Gun M1914	Fabric belt Left hand only	Air-cooled, gas operated, MMG of very early design normally mounted for field use on a tripod. Actuated by radial lever. Commercial model of gun (h) below. Originally manufactured by Colt's Patent Fire Arms Manufacturing Co to Browning Patents. (A number of these guns were manufactured by Colts during 1914–1918 for the British Government to take 0.303in ammunition; they have since been declared obsolete.)
(h)	Gun, Machine Cal .30 Colt M1914	—	Fabric belt Left hand only	Air-cooled, gas operated, MMG of very early design, normally mounted for field use on a tripod. Actuated by radial lever. Originally manufactured by Colt's Patent Fire Arms Manufacturing Co to Browning Patents. Now obsolete.
(i)	Gun, Machine Cal .30 Colt M1917	—	Fabric belt Left hand only	A later model of the Gun, Machine, Cal .30 Colt M1914 manufactured by the Marlin-Rockwell Corporation. Now obsolete.

Item	U.S. Ordnance Weapons	Commercial Weapons	Nature of feed	Remarks
(j)	Gun, Machine Cal .30 Marlin, Aircraft M1917	Colt-Marlin Aircraft Machine Gun	Metal link disintegrating belt. Left hand only.	Air-cooled, gas operated, MMG for use in fixed positions in aircraft. This is a modified Gun, Machine Cal .30 Colt M1917 actuated by horizontal piston instead of by radial lever. It has a smooth barrel without radiating fins, and an improved lock mechanism redesigned for synchronization purposes. It is fitted with a trigger motor for remote control. Developed and manufactured by the Marlin-Rockwell Corporation in 1917. (An alternative model for use as a flexible gun was developed in 1918 but not widely adopted.) Now obsolete.
(k)	Gun, Machine Cal .30 Marlin Tank M1917	Colt-Marlin Tank Machine Gun	Fabric belt Left hand only	This is the Gun, Machine Cal .30 Marlin Aircraft M1917 modified for use in tanks. It is fitted with an aluminium Lewis-type radiator, sights, a pistol grip and a hand operated trigger. Now obsolete.
(l)	—	Colt Automatic Machine Gun-Rifle Caliber MG 38 and MG 38B (Water-cooled)	(Early Models) Fabric belt. Left hand only (Later Models) Fabric belt or metal disintegrating belt. Left hand only	Watercooled, recoil operated, MMG of early design. Pistol grip rear firing control. The MG 38B is fitted with spade grips and rear trigger control. Guns MG 38 and MG 38B supplied since 1939 will function with metal link disintegrating belt as well as with fabric belt. Commercial models of guns (m) and (n) below, with which they have only limited interchangeability of parts. Obsolete.

Item	U.S. Ordnance Weapons	Commercial Weapons	Nature of feed	Remarks
(m)	Gun, Machine Cal .30 Browning M1917	—	Fabric belt. Left hand only	Watercooled, recoil operated, MMG of early design. Pistol grip rear trigger control. Designed for ground use. Now declared obsolete.
(n)	Gun, Machine Cal .30 Browning M1917 A1	—	Fabric belt. Left hand only	This is a modified Gun, Machine, Cal .30 Browning M1917 incorporating certain improvements in design, including a new bottom plate with integral elevating bracket. Standard ground gun in World War II. Obsolete.
(o)	Gun, Machine Cal .30 Browning Aircraft M1918	—	Metal disintegrating belt. Left hand only	Air-cooled, recoil operated, aircraft weapon of early design. Operating slide for charging. Fire control by trigger motor or hand type firing mechanism. Now obsolete.
(p)	Gun, Machine Cal .30 Browning Aircraft M1918 M1 (For Fixed Use Only)	—	Metal disintegrating belt. Left hand only	This is a modified model of the M1918 gun. Now obsolete.

Item	U.S. Ordnance Weapons	Commercial Weapons	Nature of feed	Remarks
(q)	Gun, Machine Cal .30 Browning Aircraft M1918 MI (For Flexible Use Only)	—	Metal disintegrating belt. Left hand only	This is a modified model of the M1918 gun, adapted for flexible use. Fitted with spade grips and rear trigger control. Has a cocking handle and no retracting slide. Now obsolete.
(r)	Gun, Machine Cal .30 Browning Aircraft M1919 Fixed and Flexible	—	Metal disintegrating belt. Left hand only	These are improved models of the M1918 MI Fixed and Flexible guns. The fixed model is provided with operating slide for charging, vertical buffer back plate and fire control by trigger motor. The flexible model is fitted with spade grips, horizontal buffer back plate, and rear trigger control. Now obsolete.
(s)		Colt Light Aircraft Machine Gun-Rifle Caliber (MG 40) (Air-Cooled). Fixed and Flexible	Metal link disintegrating belt. Left or right hand feed by rearranging the feed mechanism	Improved models of previous Browning guns designed for use in aircraft, with left or right hand feed obtainable by rearranging feed mechanism. Fixed model is provided with operating slide for charging, vertical buffer back plate and fire control by trigger motor. The flexible model is fitted with spade grips, horizontal buffer back plate, and rear trigger control. Commercial prototypes of guns (t) and (u) below, with which they have only limited interchangeability of parts. (Colt's Patent Fire Arms Manufacturing Co. produced a number of these guns modified to take 0.303in ammuni-

Item	U.S. Ordnance Weapons	Commercial Weapons	Nature of feed	Remarks
				tion for the British Government. The 0.303in model was classified as the Gun, Machine Browning. .303in Mk I. Numerous modifications subsequently carried out in England advanced the classification of this gun to Mk I Star, Mk I two Star, Mk II, and finally, by the introduction of a finned muzzle attachment, to the model Mk II Star.) Obsolete.
(t)	—	Colt Light Aircraft Machine Gun-Rifle Caliber (MG 40–2) (Fixed Type)	Metal link, disintegrating belt. Left or right hand, by rearranging the feed mechanism	This is the commercial model of the Gun, Machine, Cal .30 Browning M2 Aircraft Fixed (gun (v) below) with which it should have full interchangeability of parts. It has an operating slide for charging, a horizontal buffer back plate, and fire control by trigger motor. Interchange in direction of feed is effected by a rearrangement of the feed mechanism. Obsolete.
(u)	—	Colt Light Aircraft Machine Gun-Rifle Caliber (MG 40–2) (Flexible Type)	Metal link, disintegrating belt. Left or right hand, by rearrangement of the feed mechanism	This is the MG 40–2 Fixed model (gun (t) above) adapted for flexible use in aircraft. Fitted with spade grips, horizontal buffer back plate, and rear trigger control. Retracting slide for charging. Commercial model of Gun, Machine, Cal .30 Browning M2 Aircraft. Flexible (gun (w) below) with which it should have full interchangeability of parts. Obsolete.

Item	U.S. Ordnance Weapons	Commercial Weapons	Nature of feed	Remarks
(v)	Gun, Machine Cal .30 Browning M2 Aircraft. Fixed	—	Metal link, disintegrating belt. Left or right hand, by rearranging the feed mechanism	This is an improved type of aircraft gun, similar to the Aircraft M1919 model but narrower, lighter in weight, and modified for interchange in direction of feed. Operating slide for charging. Fire control by trigger motor. Guns of early manufacture were fitted with a vertical buffer back plate, but guns later fitted with a horizontal buffer back plate in order to make the basic back plate standard to all Cal .30 M2 Aircraft machine guns.
(w)	Gun, Machine Cal .30 Browning M2 Aircraft. Flexible	—	Metal link, disintegrating belt. Left or right hand, by rearranging the feed mechanism	This is gun (v) above adapted for flexible use in aircraft. Fitted with spade grips, horizontal buffer back plate, and rear trigger control. Retracting slide for charging.
(x)	Gun, Machine Cal .30 Browning M1919 Tank	—	Fabric belt. Left hand only	Air-cooled, recoil operated, machine gun of early design for use in tanks. Fitted with pistol grip and rear trigger control. Now obsolete.
(y)	Gun Machine Cal .30 Browning Tank, M1919 A1	—	Fabric belt. Left hand only.	This is the Tank M1919 gun provided with brackets to mount a telescopic sight. Now obsolete.

Item	U.S. Ordnance Weapons	Commercial Weapons	Nature of feed	Remarks
(z)	Gun, Machine Cal .30 Browning M1919 A2	—	Fabric belt. Left hand only.	A modified version of the Tank M1919 gun. For field and AFV use. A flexible type gun. Now obsolete. Was at one time used by the US Cavalry.
(aa)	Gun, Machine Cal .30 Browning M1919 A3	—	Fabric belt. Left hand only	This is the Tank M1919 gun with a hole drilled through the cover latch to serve as an auxiliary sight. Only a few were made.
(bb)	Gun, Machine Cal .30 Browning M1919 A4. Flexible	—	Fabric belt. Left hand only	This is an improved model of the M1919 A2 gun with length of barrel increased from 18.63in to 24in. It is fitted with the back plate of the M1919 A2 gun (see (z) above) for use in AFV's, in ground or in AA role. It has a pistol grip with rear trigger control. May be removed from the vehicle and used as a ground gun. In the field manuals this gun is sometimes termed "Browning Machine Gun Caliber .30 HB, M1919 A4". (HB indicates heavy barrel.)

Item	U.S. Ordnance Weapons	Commercial Weapons	Nature of feed	Remarks
(cc)	Gun, Machine Cal .30 Browning M1919 A4. Fixed	—	Fabric belt. Left hand only	This is the M1919 A4 Flexible model, fitted with the back plate of the M1919 Browning Aircraft fixed gun (see (r) above) to adapt it for fixed use in AFV's. A trigger grip capable of remote control is sometimes used with this gun. In the field manuals this gun is sometimes termed "Browning Machine Gun Caliber .30 HB, M1919 A4". (HB indicates heavy barrel.) Later production guns were fitted with horizontal in lieu of vertical buffer back plates.
(dd)	Gun, Machine Cal .30 Browning M1919 A5. Fixed	—	Fabric belt. Left hand only	This is the M1919 A4 Fixed model, modified for use in the Westinghouse Gyro-stabilized Tank Mounting. The modifications involved the removal of the front and rear sights, provision of a special charging slide, fitting a stud bolt in lieu of bolt handle, and drilling the right hand side plate to accommodate the fitting of the charging slide. Obsolete.
(ee)	Gun, Machine Cal .30 M2 Browning Heavy Barrel. Fixed	—	Fabric belt or metal disintegrating belt. Interchangeable left or right hand feed	This is the Gun, Machine, Cal .30 Browning M2 Aircraft Fixed. Fitted with a heavy barrel for use in AFV's so that right hand feed can be obtained. It was produced as an experimental model of which only a limited number were made, but has now been abandoned.

Item	U.S. Ordnance Weapons	Commercial Weapons	Nature of feed	Remarks
(ff)	Gun, Machine Cal .30 M2 Browning Heavy Barrel. Flexible	—	Fabric belt or metal disintegrating belt. Interchangeable left or right hand feed	This is the flexible version of fixed model gun (ee) above. It also is now abandoned.
(gg)	Gun, Machine Cal .30 Browning M1919 A6	—	Fabric belt or disintegrating metal belt	Modified M1919 A4 flexible with bipod, shoulder stock and carrying handle. Used in World War II. Now obsolete.
(hh)	Gun, Machine Cal .30 Browning M1919 A4 E1	—	Fabric belt or disintegrating metal belt	Post World War II development of the M1919 A4 with retracting slide similar to M1919 A5. Never in Service.

CHAPTER SIX

Other American Machine Guns

AFTER MAXIM and Browning had shown the practicability of a fully automatic machine gun, a large number of inventors set out to make fame and fortune for themselves by producing weapons which although not infringing the patents already registered, made use of the principle established therein. As a result the period 1900–1910 brought out many weapons, some of which were tried, many of which never got off the drawing board. However there were so many of these guns that space alone must limit mention to those that were taken into service.

The Lewis Gun

The Lewis gun was designed by Col Isaac N. Lewis—a Regular officer of the United States Army. He was born in New Salem, Pennsylvania on October 12, 1858 and moved to Kansas with his parents, whilst still young. He graduated from the USA Military Academy in 1884 and for the next 25 years he was engaged on Coast Artillery matters. In 1910 the Automatic Arms Co of Buffalo, NY asked him to develop patents originated by Samuel McClean for a light machine gun. In 1911 Lewis had produced five working models which he fired at Fort Myer to demonstrate the gun to the Secretary of War, General Wood the Chief of Army Staff, and various ordnance officers. After these firings, four weapons were handed to the Board of Ordnance. Here began a most extraordinary sequence of controversy between Lewis and the American Ordnance Board. Since the Board, it seemed, would not make a decision about the gun, Lewis took back his four guns and came to Europe. A company was formed in Liège to manufacture the gun but BSA took over the entire production and when war broke out in 1914 the entire capacity of BSA was put on to the Lewis gun. To increase supplies the Savage Arms Corporation of Utica, New York, started making the arm under contract and in 1917 was producing 400 guns a week. When America came into the war Savage started to supply the US Forces and produced 34 000 before the Armistice.

During World War I the gun was used in Europe by the British, Belgium and Italian armies in vast numbers. It was a light weight, air cooled gas operated gun holding 47 rounds in a flat drum magazine mounted on a post on top of the gun. The piston was racked on the underside and the teeth connected with a clock type spring mechanism which was wound up as the piston came back and provided the energy to drive the piston and bolt forward. The bolt was mounted on the piston post and had a hollow interior. A cam slot was cut in the bolt so that the piston post drove the bolt forward and then rotated it to lock into the body before the striker fixed to the post went on to fire the cartridge. The gun mechanism rotated the drum and placed a round in front of the bolt ready for chambering. The major source of trouble came from the two spring loaded pawls which in one case allowed rotation of the magazine and in the other prevented contra-rotation. These were prone to breakage.

The Lewis gun was an extremely good infantry gun and, in fact, after the war it remained the standard British Infantry Section gun until replaced by the Bren gun in 1939. But its major claim to fame is as an aircraft gun.

On June 7, 1912 Lt Col Lewis persuaded—if in fact he needed persuading—the Commanding Officer at the US Army experimental flying station at College Park just outside Washington, to take a Lewis machine gun up in his aeroplane and fire it at a ground target. The aircraft was a Type B Wright pusher. The pilot and observer rested their feet on a cross-bar and it was over this bar that the gun was placed. The CO who took up the gun was Captain Chandler and his pilot was Lt T. Milling. The target was a piece of white cloth 6ft by 7ft laid flat on the ground. The plane flew over at 250ft and Capt Chandler fired a short burst. After three such passes Capt Chandler shot off the rest of the pan in a nearby pond so that he could observe the fall of shot. There were five hits on the cloth and bullet scars on the ground in front.

Next day Chandler and Milling flew over a target 18yd long by 2yd wide at 550ft. They fired 44 shots and there were 14 hits. A local photographer named MacCartee photographed the plane with the gun but had to be content with a substitute pilot as Lt Milling was away on the day he arrived.

The military authorities played this down and insisted that the idea of air battles was sheer nonsense—airplanes were to gather information not to fight.

The first demonstration in Europe of firing a Lewis from an aircraft took place at Brasschaet in Belgium in December 1912. On November 27, 1913 a Lewis was used again from a Graham White bi-plane over Bisley.

On August 22, 1914 two British pilots named Lt L. Strange and Lt Penn Gaskell took a Lewis gun up in their aircraft and shot at a

German Albatross at 5 000 ft. They reported their feat but received scant encouragement to repeat it.

Fairly soon after this the practice of using a Lewis gun on a free mounting became widespread. It was very suitable for this task and when fitted with a double drum of 96 rounds, as had occurred during the Battle of the Somme in 1916, it had adequate ammunition. The shoulder butt was removed and spade grips substituted. It should be noted that the Lewis gun was not suitable for synchronisation to enable it to shoot through the propeller. This was because the gun fired from the open breech position. When the trigger was pulled, the sear which was engaged in a bent in the piston, was released and the piston went forward carrying the bolt which fed and chambered the round before rotating to lock. All this took time—probably about 30 milli-seconds— and also varied in this time depending upon whether the gun was pointing upwards which increased the time or downwards where gravity helped. So for synchronisation a short response time was essential and closed breech firing weapons such as the Vickers were used.

The Lewis guns were extremely successful in the defence of England against the Zeppelins. Using yellow phosphorus incendiary ammunition developed by George Buckingham, they destroyed 10 Zeppelins out of the 12 known to be shot down over London.

The American army largely ignored the Lewis. The Navy were interested and the Marines went to France fully equipped with the gun—but as soon as they came under Army control the Lewis's were withdrawn. There have been many attempts to explain this. Some have maintained a clash of personalities between Lewis and General Crozier, the Chief of Ordnance, was the root cause. There is one possible explanation. The original four guns submitted for trial in 1911 were considered to be harsh in their action and the bolt was accelerated so rapidly to the rear that the extractor often tore through the rim of the case. This was caused by unlocking the bolt too early. This came about because the straight portion of the cam path cut in the bolt for the piston post to operate in was not long enough. The original length was 0.875in but when BSA started manufacture they increased this to 1.0625in. This gave a longer period of mechanical safety and by delaying the moment of breech unlocking also reduced the rate of fire to about 600 rounds/minute. All American Army information was limited to the original four guns and no trials were conducted either into the performance of the BSA gun or that manufactured by Savage.

Col Lewis declined to accept any royalties on the Lewis guns bought by the United States and paid to the Treasury over $1m he received from the manufacturers. This patriotic gesture brought a disparaging response from Gen Crozier so perhaps after all it was entirely a matter of personalities.

After Dunkirk the Americans sold Britain 1 157 Lewis guns which were used for Home Guard, Anti-aircraft and Merchant Navy ships defence. All of these were .3 calibre and can occasionally be met in museums marked with the red line indicating the .30–06 round.

From purely technical considerations the most interesting feature of the Lewis gun was undoubtedly the cooling system. The barrel could not easily be changed in the field and the heat produced when firing was dissipated from the barrel via aluminium vanes contained in a light steel casing. The designer's claim was that as the gun fired the expanding gases at the muzzle drew cold air in through the casing from the breech end towards the muzzle and so cooled the barrel. The secret was said to lie in the induced air flow. Unfortunately the aircraft guns and most of the Savage guns had neither vanes nor casing and yet they dissipated heat perfectly well when fired on the ground! It seems whole generations of infantrymen carried a gun which could well have been reduced by a further 4lb.

The Johnson Machine Gun

Melvin M. Johnson, born in Boston in 1909, went to Harvard University and Harvard Law School; he produced a prototype light machine gun in 1937 chambered for the .30–06 round which was tested by the Marine Corps in 1941. This gun had several unusual features. The barrel recoiled to produce unlocking of the bolt and the energy required by the bolt to carry out the cycle of operations came from blowback. The barrel only recoiled $\frac{1}{8}$in and the bolt was freed with a higher chamber pressure than usual, 1 000–1 500lbf/in². This led to a very brisk bolt movement and a fairly high rate of fire. The 20 round magazine fitted horizontally into the gun from the left and could be topped up through a latch on the right hand side of the body—using chargers. The gun fired single shot from a closed breech and full auto from an open breech. This gave the short delay between trigger operation and cap initiation that is essential for accurate single shot firing and also allowed open breech operation to cool the chamber between bursts. This open breech system leaves the next round to be fired in the magazine until the bolt goes forward, to fire, and in this way the risk of a cook off is eliminated.

The gun was used by the Marines in the Pacific and the Army's First Special Service force in Italy. About 5 000 guns were produced.

In December 1943 Johnson came up with an improved machine gun. It was tested but found to be too susceptible to dirty operating conditions.

P.H.M.G.—E

The M60 Machine Gun

At the end of the Second World War the American Army had the BAR and various models of Browning machine gun, all excellent weapons but dating back to before the First World War. The doctrine of the General Purpose machine gun was also in current fashion. This it will be recalled, is a machine gun light enough to be carried by one man in the Infantry Section but capable when mounted on a tripod of producing sustained fire.

The NATO powers had agreed to standardise on the 7.62mm × 51 round which although smaller than the .30–60 was still a big powerful round capable of producing effective machine gun fire from a suitable gun out to a range exceeding 2 000 metres.

The USA Army put in a great deal of work to produce this machine gun. They produced several new guns and did the necessary work to convert existing guns if it should be necessary, to take the new cartridge known then as the T65E2. It became clear in about 1956 that the T161E3 would be the gun and this was adopted with the nomenclature of M60.

This gun uses pressings and stampings in its construction together with rubber and plastics in place of more orthodox materials. It is a gas operated gun with a constant energy gas cut-off system. This is so arranged that gas comes from a tapping near the muzzle and passes through holes in the *side* of a piston. When enough energy has been given to the piston it starts to move and by so doing the holes in the piston wall move away from the gas supply and cut it off. In theory this system needs no gas regulator because increased friction caused by dirt, sand, carbon etc. merely holds up piston movement until additional gas arrives to supply the energy required. In practice if the piston cannot be accelerated by the first impulsive blow produced by the gas, then it may never receive enough energy to move. The belt feed system is taken directly from the German MG 42 (see page 101) and the piston and bolt are taken without modification from the German FG 42 (see page 102). The barrel change arrangements are not good with a hot barrel and each barrel carries its own bipod and gas cylinder which makes a considerable increase to the weight carried by those members of the section carrying spare barrels and of course puts up the cost of the gun.

On the other hand the barrel has a very well constructed stellite liner which is much longer than any liner the Belgians or British have been able to make and as a result its barrel accuracy life is much more.

The arrangements for zeroing the barrels are not good. As a barrel wears and loses muzzle velocity it requires an increased elevation to achieve a given range. Since an air cooled gun will often have three barrels it is essential that all zeroing—ie adjusting the sights so that the line of fire intercepts the line of sight at the required range—should be done on the barrel, and then changing the barrel automatically means fitting a zeroed barrel. On the M60 all zeroing is done on the back sight of the gun. The complications of this must be obvious to all!

The M60 is the universal US ground gun and has been used in South Viet-Nam for some years. It has also been purchased by the Australians and New Zealanders who have also used it there.

It is not generally regarded as a gun which does credit to the immense design and construction skill available in the USA.

The M73 Tank Gun

A co-axially mounted tank machine gun has requirements that differ from a ground gun. Firstly it is used in a confined space and the design must ensure that no fumes emerge from the breech or the gas system— if it is gas operated—otherwise the crew of the armoured fighting vehicle would rapidly be asphyxiated. Secondly there is very little room in a tank turret so the gun must have as short an inboard length as possible. Next the barrel change must be accomplished entirely within the turret and it is therefore very inconvenient to have to remove the old barrel in a forward direction as this necessitates the entire gun being first drawn back into the turret. Lastly, the gun should be capable, with the minimum of changing of parts, of feeding its belt through from either side.

From the performance viewpoint it must have the characteristics of a medium machine gun and be capable of firing long bursts without loss of accuracy.

The Browning tank machine gun, although an extremely good gun, was of course chambered for the .30–06 round and also had a long receiver which occupied valuable space, and after the war ended in 1945 a new design was started. After a lot of early work it was decided to adapt a gun designed by Mr. Russel Robinson, an Australian who brought a design to England in 1948 and worked on it at the Royal Small Arms Factory at Enfield. For various reasons it was not adopted here and he went to America where his design was investigated. It was initially given the number T197E2 and subsequently became the M73.

It is a recoil operated gun and therefore with no gas system it will not produce exhaust fumes. The rate of fire has been kept down to 450–500 rounds a minute to ensure that the breech is kept closed as long as possible to clear the chamber of fumes before the cartridge case emerges.

To keep the inboard length short it has a sliding, sideways operating, breech block and so the round does not have the length of a conventional breech block behind it to ram it into the chamber. This keeps the inboard length down to $11\frac{1}{2}$in whereas the Browning with a reciprocating block has an inboard length of $15\frac{3}{4}$in.

The gun can readily be belt fed—using the same disintegrating link belt as the M60 and nearly all other NATO machine guns—from either side.

The body of the gun can be pivoted either to the left or to the right and the barrel drawn straight back into the crew compartment for changing. This idea was first used in the German MG 34 (qv) and makes barrel changing a simple operation (*59*).

However this short body has produced a complicated mechanism. When the barrel recoils a simple cam path forces the very small breech across to the right. The extractor pulls the case back and transfers it to a carrier which then pivots downward and revolves the case so that it is pointing forwards below the barrel. When the rammer drives the next round into the chamber, the empty case is pushed forward into a receptacle which prevents it falling on the floor and getting under foot. This process of extraction and ejection has in the past been suspect and for this reason the gun was not accepted for the British Chieftain tank. Development of the gun was a lengthy process and a lot of changes were incorporated before it reached its present stage where it is used in the current American M60 tank.

Another advantage the M73 has over the Browning is that whereas the top cover plate of the latter lifts upwards and requires a lot of headroom, the M73 cover can be opened sideways and takes up less room above the gun. A version of the gun has been produced that can be dismantled and used on a tripod in the ground role.

The M85 .5 calibre Tank Machine Gun

This gun was developed to replace the .5 Browning M2 by the Aircraft Armament Corporation. It was originally known as the T175E2. The requirement was for a gun suitable for co-axial mounting or being used on top of the turret as a commander's gun for both ground and air targets. The requirement for ground targets is a rate of fire of about 400 rounds a minute with .5 calibre but against aircraft the need is about 1 000 rounds a minute so the gun has a choice of these two rates of fire.

The gun is recoil operated with a unique method of transferring energy to the breech block using a pivoted stirrup rather than the conventional accelerator as used on the Browning. The stirrup accelerates the bolt carrier and after a short period the bolt is unlocked from the carrier and continues to the rear to carry out a conventional cycle of operations.

The slow rate of fire is achieved by having a rotating delay drum which is struck by the recoiling bolt. This causes the solenoid plunger to release the sear which rises and holds up the bolt on its feed stroke. The drum continues to revolve, winding up a spring. When it reaches the end of its rotation the spring causes counter rotation and it returns to release the solenoid plunger which in turn lowers the sear and the bolt goes forward to feed, chamber and lock. The gun can be fired either electrically or manually and can also be dismounted and fired from a tripod.

GEC Guns

The International General Electric Company of New York have produced a number of guns based on the Gatling principle of revolving barrels, electrically powered. The 20mm version is the M61 Vulcan which is used in a large number of fighter aircraft including the Phantom. This gun fires at 4 000 rounds a minute and produces a converging cone of fire which is ideal for aircraft use where the time of engagement is short.

This gun has also been used as the basis of a ground anti-aircraft system which is either mounted on a self propelled chassis or alternatively towed. With on-mounted radar it produces a highly accurate lethal system for the protection of convoys, gun positions and vital points. It also has great application to ship borne use for employment against surface skimming missiles.

The war in Viet-Nam brought the helicopter into use on a scale never seen before. The armoured helicopter was devised not only to protect the similar craft carrying troops but with a fixed rotor, as a genuine attacking gun-ship capable of neutralising areas on the ground. To do this GEC developed the mini-gun which is a 7.62mm version of the Vulcan weighing basically only 35lb, firing up to 6 000 rounds a minute and again electrically powered. This was fitted to the Bell Hueycobra and the Cheyenne.

A number of experimental guns on the Gatling system including a 3 barrel 30mm cannon have also been developed.

The .223 (5.56mm) Machine Guns

When the .223 Remington cartridge was developed by Eugene Stoner of the Armalite Division of Fairchild Airplane and Engine Corporation for the AR-15 rifle, design and development started on a number of machine gun projects.

Stoner himself left Armalite in 1961 to become a consultant with Colt's Patent Firearms Co at Hartford. He then devised a system of guns based on a common body, breech block, return spring, and trigger mechanism to which could be added a series of barrels and butts to make a family consisting of: Sub-machine gun, rifle, LMG, MMG, and a vehicle fixed gun. This family was known as the Stoner 63 system. Subsequently it was modified into the Stoner 63A system in which there were two series, one based on the rifle and the other on the machine gun. The Stoner 63A Light machine gun exists both as a magazine fed gun and as a belt fed weapon. The LMG, magazine fed, weighs only $11\frac{1}{2}$ pounds and is of orthodox gas operation employing a gas piston. It has a rapid barrel change and would appear to be an effective arm out to about 500–600 metres. Its rate of fire must however be limited to about 60 rounds a minute over any prolonged period due to barrel heating problems.

The 63A belt fed LMG has been designed in its latest version to be belt fed from the right. The direction of feed was recently changed by Cadillac Gage who manufacture in USA and NWM Kruithoorn of s'Hertgenbosh who make it in Holland, to prevent the ammunition box bumping the leg of a right handed soldier carrying it by the handle. The barrel has been made somewhat heavier and the bipod which now folds along the handguard, is detachable. The gun is designated the Stoner 63A1 and is in fact a very accurate weapon. With two barrels it can fire at 80 rounds a minute for a prolonged period and of course, produce a much higher rate for short lengths of time. The US Army are now testing this gun as the XM22, the Navy as the Mk. 23.

The Colt Patent Firearms Corp. have produced a number of LMGs based on the AR-15 rifle. The most promising of these is the CAR which is basically the AR-15 with a heavy barrel and bipod and a 30 round magazine.

GEC also came into the .223 field with a fast firing gun which was a scaled down version of the mini-gun. This was made in prototype and successfully passed its tests. It fired at a rate of up to 10 000 rounds a minute and demonstrated a burst length of 2 600 rounds at 6 700 rounds/minute and a malfunction rate of 25 000 rounds per misfire.

Like all the GEC revolving multi-barrel guns there is no misfire problem as the misfired round is ejected from the gun, no cook-off problem as there is automatic clearing after each burst but a hang fire is a hazard.

Future Development

The main effort in the recent past has been to produce a round giving a lower impulse to the weapon and thus allowing a light weight arm which can be fired at a high rate without the muzzle rising drastically. Future work could well be aimed at producing an even lighter projectile and departing from spin stabilised flight to fin stabilised. The

light weight flechette has been tried over the last few years and development continues to improve its accuracy.

With a 10 grain flechette the firing impulse would be small indeed
and with a burst fire control giving three rounds for every trigger pull,
the future light machine gun could weigh as little as 8lb.

A photograph of the flechette and the Aircraft Armament Incorporated gun are at (72–74).

CHAPTER SEVEN

British Machine Guns

IT IS SAD to have to say that throughout the long history of machine guns in the British service there has never been one of British design actually adopted.

In February 1867 the Ordnance Select Committee—forerunner of the modern Ordnance Board—tested the Gatling gun. It is obvious that the tactical role of the gun was not clearly defined because the comparative firings conducted were between the Gatling and the 9 pounder breech loader and the results were assessed by the number of hits obtained by the Gatling and the number of perforations of the targets achieved by the shrapnel balls of the field pieces. As a result of this the Committee recommended that no decision be taken to introduce a machine gun at that time.

In 1869 Major George Fosbery, VC, who was employed by the India Office went to Brussels and witnessed a trial of the original Montigny gun upon which he commented favourably. When the Montigny mitrailleuse was adopted by the French Army in 1869 the War Office set up a special committee in August of that year which tried out the Gatling and the Montigny. The first report in late October 1870 recommended that the Gatling should be adopted and 12 .45 Gatlings were purchased for the Army and 12 .45 Gatlings and 24 .65 Gatlings for the Navy.

The Committee then carried out further trials of the Gatlings of .45 and .65 calibre, the Montigny, the 9pdr ML and 12pdr BL firing shrapnel and segment shell and infantry sections firing the Snider and Martini Henry. The firings were conducted at ranges from 300 to 2 100yd. In general the Gatling produced much the best results at close ranges and even at 2 070yd obtained 164 hits against 115 hits from shrapnel fired by the BLR 12pdr.* The Committee also interviewed officers who had been with the French and German armies during the Franco-Prussian War. The Committee issued a second report in 1871, confirming its previous view and proposed further that the .65 Gatling should be adopted for the Navy and for Coast Defence and the .45 for the Army.

---

*Capt. Owen, Captain Instructor at the Royal Gun Factory, Woolwich, a member of the Committee published these figures in a pamphlet "Compound Guns, Many Barrelled Rifle Batteries, Machine Guns or Mittrailleuse", London 1874

The first Gatlings were delivered by Sir W. G. Armstrong and Co, in January 1874 and by the end of 1875 40 guns of .45 calibre were produced. The 12 .45in guns originally destined for the Army were taken by the Navy who could see a practical need for the gun (*14*).

Interest was then shown by the Navy in the Nordenfelt and trials were carried out in 1877 at HMS Excellent, Portsmouth. The Navy asked for 50 Nordenfelts to replace 50 Gatlings and for a suitable mobile carriage to be designed. These were produced by Messrs Temple and Co, who were licensed by Nordenfelt for UK manufacture.

The War Office put out a requirement in 1879 for a machine gun to be capable of: (1) Firing the solid drawn case cartridge of .45 calibre used by the .45 Gatling (2) Land and naval service (3) Being operated by not more than 3 men, firing 200 rounds in 30sec, and firing at a "rapid rate" for not less than 1 000 rounds. In March 1881 the following guns were tested: Gatling 6 barrel—cranked from the side; Gatling 10 barrel—cranked from the rear (direct action); Gatling 10 barrel—cranked from the side; Nordenfelt 10 barrel; Nordenfelt 5 barrel; Gardner 2 barrel and Gardner 5 barrel; Pratt and Whitney (improved Gardner) 4 barrel. The stipulation of 3 man crews was relaxed for this trial.

The 4 barrelled 1in Nordenfelt Mks I and II had already come into Naval Service in July 1880 and following the trial the Gardner in 2 and 5 barrels was adopted in 1884 and the single barrel version was purchased in limited numbers in 1885.

From this it can be seen that the Navy was far more alive to the use of the machine gun than was the Army and as a result many of the Army operations were supported by Naval machine gun detachments.

In 1886 the Adjutant-General requested that a galloping carriage be developed. This led to some interesting and—in our modern eyes— amusing results. It should be noted that in spite of War Office indifference the volunteers had shown great interest in the machine gun and had produced at their own expense various forms of carriage. "Colonel Alt* of the Central London Rangers (Volunteers) 22nd Middlesex Regiment who designed a magazine carriage on which was mounted, above wheel level, a Nordenfelt rifle calibre machine gun in 1884, brought the Battalion machine gun section of two guns into the field on manoeuvres. The gun had 5 barrels and the caisson held 5 000 rounds of .45in ammunition. The Cyclist Battalion of the 26th Middlesex Regiment invented a light carriage for the Maxim drawn as a trailer by 2 cyclists" (*32*).

The Regular Cavalry also bought carriages at the CO's expense and

Machine Guns by Lt Col Hutchinson

Lt Col Liddell of the 10th Hussars equipped his Regiment with horse drawn galloping carriages for the Nordenfelt.

The advent and development of the Maxim gun and the formation of the Maxim Gun Company in 1884 with Albert Vickers as Chairman, introduced the first true machine gun to the British service. The Maxim gun was first purchased in 1887 and was adopted on a scale of one instructional gun per Battalion in 1890 but instruction in the Gardner and Nordenfelt went on at Hythe until 1894 and even in 1897 each Battalion had not yet received its Maxim gun.

When the Boer War came the Maxim could have been used to great effect but its reputation was not enhanced by poor tactical handling, poorly trained troops and the use of the high wheeled carriage. The Boers used the Maxim pom-pom to great effect. "In the British assault at Cronje's Laager at Paardberg the machine guns of the Scots Guards at Modder River remained out of action all day, the teams in the firing line having been annihilated by Boer pom-pom fire."*

In 1909 machine gun sections in the Battalion got two guns for training. Regular Battalions got Mk IV tripods and a limbered wagon, Territorials got the Infantry Carriage Mk III with 4ft 8in wheels.

It is worthwhile digressing for a moment to mention Lt Col N. R. McMahon of the Royal Fusiliers who was Chief Instructor at the School of Infantry at Hythe. He gave a lecture entitled "Fire Tactics" on December 18 ,1907 to the Aldershot Military Society and the lecture was so impressive that the British Field Service Regulations and Training Manuals were re-written to incorporate his views. Whilst these regulations were still in the draft stage they were communicated to the German Military Attaché in exchange for "other official information" and they reached the German General Staff who promptly embodied them in their own Field Service Regulations.†

The British Army was so little interested in the machine gun that Colonel McMahon was compelled to concentrate the training at Hythe on the rifleman. It was largely due to his "mad minute" and inspired training that we sent the finest infantry shots ever found in any army to France with the 1914 Expeditionary Force.‡

Colonel McMahon was promoted to Brigadier-General in France in 1914 but was killed by a shell burst at Ypres before he assumed command of 10 Infantry Brigade.

The Vickers Gun
The basic action of the Maxim was amended at Crayford by turning

* *The Times History of the War in South Africa*
† *Machine Guns by Lt Col G. S. Hutchinson*
‡ *Superiority of Fire by Major Pridham*

the crank to break upwards and putting the trigger bar on the top. It came into British Service in November 1912 and remained in continuous use until the 1960s. It is still in use in some forces.

The Vickers gun served the British Army well. It was a water cooled gun holding 7 pints in the jacket around the barrel. The water boiled after 600 rounds fired at 200 rounds a minute. The boiling water improved the heat transfer due to the convection currents set up. Water evaporated at the rate of $1\frac{1}{2}$ pints per 1 000 rounds after commencing to boil. The steam was led off through the steam tube and the condenser hose (76) to the condenser can. The water condensed in the can was poured back into the jacket.

The barrel could be changed when worn out after 10 000 rounds at 200 rounds a minute—or after an hour's continuous firing. The process involved elevating the gun, pulling the barrel back and inserting a cork into the jacket, depressing the gun and withdrawing the barrel. The new barrel had been previously prepared by wrapping asbestos string in the grooves to make a water tight gland and it was inserted from the rear. The muzzle pushed out the cork in the hole in the front of the jacket and the barrel sealed the holes. The gun was depressed to drain the water out of the barrel and was then ready for a further 10 000 rounds in the next hour before another barrel change would be required. Using the Mk VIIIZ streamlined bullet the gun could provide deadly fire on to reverse slopes and enemy forming up places, as much as 4 500yd away.

The gun performed some extraordinary feats in both World Wars. The following account from the official history of the Machine Gun Corps is an example.

"In a further attack upon High Wood on August 24, 1916, a somewhat amazing exploit was carried out by the 100th Machine Gun Company. Ten guns were grouped in Savoy Trench, from which a magnificent view was obtained of the German line at a range of about 2 000yd. Two companies of infantry were lent for the purpose of carrying ammunition and water to the battery position during the previous night, when the machine guns were installed, and camouflaged with netting. The operation orders read that 'rapid fire is to be maintained continuously for twelve hours to cover the attack and consolidation'.

"During the attack on August 24, 250 rounds short of one million were fired by the ten guns. Four 2-gallon petrol tins of water, the company's water-bottles, and all the urine tins from the neighbourhood were emptied into the guns for cooling purposes, an illustration of the amount of water consumed; while a party was employed throughout the action carrying ammunition. Strict discipline as to barrel-changing was maintained. The company artificer, assisted by one private, maintained a belt filling machine in action without cessation for twelve hours. A prize of five francs to each of the members of the gun-team firing the greatest number of rounds was secured by the gun-teams of Sergeant P. Dean, DCM* with a record of just over 120,000 rounds.

"*Later Major P. Dean, MC, DCM now of the Royal Tank Corps."

The .303in Vickers served through two world wars and was used on the ground, in the air and at sea. The .5 Vickers also played a great part in tanks, aircraft and ships. The various marks of Vickers are of interest to enthusiasts only and are shown as an appendix to this chapter.

The Lewis Gun

The British army originally got the Lewis gun because production of the Vickers was inadequate, but it introduced a completely different conception of machine gun employment. It weighed 30lb with its 47 round drum magazine and was fired off a bipod. It was carried and fired by one man which made it an extremely mobile source of fire power.

When in the autumn of 1915 Vickers guns were withdrawn from Infantry Battalions and Brigaded, four Lewis guns were issued instead. By June 1916 this number had reached 8 guns per Battalion, ie 2 guns per company, and in the autumn it became one per platoon. In 1918 each platoon got another gun and 4 were held at Bn HQ for AA work. Battalions that started the war with two Maxims thus ended four years later with 36 Lewis guns.*

The Lewis gun was the standard Infantry section gun until replaced by the Bren. It was not only a ground gun but was used extensively in the air and at sea. It came to the rescue of our depleted weapon stores after Dunkirk and continued to give sterling value at sea until the end of World War II. The various marks are shown (*45–53*) and in the table at the end of the book.

The Beardmore-Farquhar Machine Gun

The first British designed weapon to receive serious consideration was the Beardmore-Farquhar machine gun. This was designed by Colonel Mowbray Gore Farquhar, manufactured by Beardmore in Birmingham and tested by the RAF in November 1919. The gun was of very unusual design. It was gas operated but instead of the gas piston working directly to the bolt it compressed a spring as it was forced rearwards by gas pressure until the piston moved over a sear and was held with the spring fully compressed. When the pressure of the gas in the chamber was high the bolt head was locked against locking lugs in the body

Machine Guns by Lt Col Hutchinson

and as soon as the pressure dropped the force of the spring unlocked the bolt and carried it to the rear—at the same time compressing a bolt closing spring. When the bolt came back it extracted and ejected the empty case. The main return spring had expended its energy by then and the bolt closing spring was able to force the bolt forward to feed, chamber and lock. So in brief the principle was that the locked bolt remained locked until the force required to unlock it was less than the strength of the compressed main spring.

The gun was very lightly constructed with the minimum of body enclosure and since it was an aircraft gun and not exposed to mud and sand this was sound enough. It weighed only $16\frac{1}{4}$lb with a 77 round double drum magazine.

The test was very successful. The gun fired at all angles of elevation and depression and with the plane imposing additional g forces on the system. The springs made the action very much smoother than the conventional gas piston action and it fired 320 rounds at 18 000ft with one stoppage caused by a bad round. However it came too late and with retrenchment the order of the day the RAF did not take it up and no more was heard of it.

The BSA Machine Gun

During World War I the Birmingham Small Arms Co produced all the Lewis guns used by the armed services. After the war they produced a private venture .5in calibre aircraft gun (*121*). This was a recoil operated gun of unusual design. The barrel, breech block and carrier all recoiled together for $2\frac{7}{8}$in until the carrier was cammed round to unlock the bolt. The barrel was returned by its own spring and the bolt and carrier continued rearwards and the empty case was ejected downwards. The bolt and carrier were held to the rear until, when the barrel had fully run out, they were released to come forward, feed a round from the 37 round magazine, chamber it, lock and fire.

The long recoil of the locked barrel and bolt kept the rate of fire to 400 rounds a minute which was very slow for an aircraft gun and this plus the very limited ammunition supply caused its rejection when tested in 1928.

The Vickers Berthier Machine Gun

This gun strictly speaking could hardly be called a British design since the original Berthier gun was French but the manufacturing rights were acquired by Vickers and in 1925 they kept the Crayford plant in work by limited manufacture of the gun. It was a gas operated gun with a piston underneath the barrel serving a tilting block. It was a very smoothly operating gun and was adopted by the Indian Army in 1933

to replace the Hotchkiss and Lewis. The Mk I and Mk II were manufactured by Vickers and the Mk III by the Rifle Factory at Ishapore.
There was a lot of argument in the early 1930s as to whether the gun
should be adopted for the British Army. The British officers of the
Indian Army swore by it but Whitehall was not quite so enthusiastic.

An aircraft version known as the Vickers Gas Operated gun was made
in 1928 and the RAF tried it. It fired at 900 rounds a minute and was
extremely simple to service in the air. The barrel could be changed in
five seconds and the ejector and extractor could be changed without
stripping the gun.

British Aircraft Armament

In the early 1930s the RAF stood in need of a new generation of aircraft.
In 1931 an RAF pilot had flown at over 400mph in a Schneider trophy
plane and from this design came the high speed fighters of the Battle of
Britain. These planes required a reliable gun with a high rate of fire
to ensure maximum target effect during the short time of engagement
available. The Vickers gun and the Lewis gun firing at 500 rounds a
minute were adequate for the 100mph fighters of World War I but now
what was required was a reliable gun firing at least 1 000 rounds a
minute.

To find the best available fixed gun the RAF held a comparative
trial in 1934 at Martlesham Heath. The guns tested were the Colt
Commercial aircraft machine gun, the MG 40—basically the American
Browning M2 gun—the French Darne, the Danish Madsen, the Hungarian Kirali and the Vickers Central Action. These guns are illustrated
later in the book. There was no consideration given to a cannon
although the Hispano-Suiza 20mm gun was already mounted between
the cylinder banks of French aircraft, firing through the propeller boss.

There was no doubt whatsoever which gun was the best. The Colt
proved its superiority and was adopted. The Air Ministry sent out
tenders to all and sundry but BSA were not included. Sir Geoffrey
Burton, Chairman of the firm approached the Ministry and was told
that BSA made bicycles, this was not their sort of work. He pointed out
that every Lewis gun made in this country—totalling 145 397—had
come from the Birmingham Small Arms Factories.* BSA got the order
and their guns played a major part in the battles over Britain in 1940.

Similarly there was a need for an observer's gun. The power operated
turret was not in service and a manually operated fast firing gun was
needed. The weapons tested in September 1934 were the Vickers Gas
Operated gun, the French Darne, the Finnish Lahti, the French

The Other Battle by Donovan M. Ward

Hotchkiss observer's gun and the BSA Adams Willmot gun. Photographs of all the guns are given later. The Vickers Gas Operated gun was the best but due to the advent of the power operated turret which could take a belt fed gun, it was not procured in large numbers.

The Bren Gun

The British Army continued using the Lewis gun after World War I. Not until 1932 was anything done about a replacement and in that year a number of trials were held of possible successors. The most favoured gun was the Vickers-Berthier already in service with the Indian Army and manufactured by Vickers; another gun tried was the Danish Madsen, a weapon of considerable complexity but steadily developed since 1902, and used by a large number of countries as well as Denmark and Norway. However the British Military Attaché had attended a demonstration of a Czechoslovakian light machine gun called the Zb26 and he wrote to Whitehall full of praise. Surprisingly the Whitehall pundits listened and this gun was also tried.

The tests were prolonged and exhaustive but there was little doubt that the Czech gun was the best weapon. The Zb26 was chambered for the Mauser 7.92mm rimless round and the British round was the rimmed .303 so a certain amount of re-design was required. At the same time the barrel was shortened and the gas tapping moved from near the muzzle towards the breech. At the same time it was considered that the finning on the barrel gave only a marginal improvement in heat transfer and harboured dirt and oil which would burn off to produce a heat haze over the sights.

In retrospect this would have been a good opportunity to get rid of the rimmed round which was always a potential source of stoppages because if badly loaded into the magazine the rims could overlap and cause jamming. The 7.92mm round was very good and in fact at this time a 7.92mm rifle was available. However it is suspected that the Treasury vetoed the change because we had ample stocks of rifles and .303 ammunition.

The Czech designers Vaclav Holek and Anton Marek produced a prototype to the British requirement known as the ZGB. This had the changes mentioned and also the shape of the butt was altered to allow use of the British overhand grip of the small of the butt (as opposed to the Continental underhand grip). A soft buffer was added to allow the barrel and body to move rearwards on firing to cushion the firing impulse.

It was decided that the gun should be made at Enfield and to this end Mr F. G. Robinson, the Factory Superintendent, planned the method of production, installed a very large number of machine tools and the drawing office was set to work. Some measure of the immensity of the task* can be gathered from the fact that there were 270 operations on the body of the gun alone and for this component 550 gauges were required each made to an accuracy of 0.0005in. It was virtually impossible to do much until the final drawings—dimensioned in inches as opposed to the Continental millimetres—were received. They arrived in January 1935 and in September 1937 the first gun was assembled. This was an achievement of which any manufacturer could have been proud and reflects very favourably on the Royal Small Arms Factory. By December 1937 42 guns were completed and by July 1938 production was 300 a week. In September 1939 the rate was 400 a week. Enfield was the sole UK manufacturer and the effects of one bombing raid would have been catastrophic.

The name BREN comes from the first two letters of **BR**NO and the first two of **ENF**IELD.

Magazines were produced by BSA and Austin. These gave a lot of trouble because it was found that they would only function with 29 rounds instead of 30. This was traced eventually to a drawing error because the magazines had been designed for rimless cartridges.

The Bren gun was also manufactured by Inglis in Canada in .303 calibre for Britain and 7.92mm for the Chinese. By 1943 Canada was making 60 per cent of the Bren guns.

There is no doubt that the Bren was one of, if not the most efficient light machine gun used during World War II. It was the standard weapon of all the British forces, the Indian Army, and was used by the Poles in Italy, the Free French and in fact appeared in almost every theatre including S.E. Asia where the Australians used it.

After the war it was re-chambered for the NATO 7.62mm × 51 round, and re-named the L4. It is still in service with units other than Infantry. A table of Bren marks is at the end of the book.

The BESAL Gun

The production of the Bren gun at Enfield meant that one successful enemy air attack at the commencement of the war would leave the army with no light machine guns and so BSA were asked to produce prototypes of a replacement gun based on the simplest pattern and designed for rapid production.

The chief designer, Harry Faulkoner, produced the BESAL. It was a gas operated gun with a simple rectangular block. Locking was achieved by a ramp on the piston forcing up two projecting lugs which

*Machinery—June 23, 30, July 7, 14 and 21, 1938.

entered locking recesses in the top of the body. The block therefore did not tilt like that of the Bren. The return spring was located under the barrel, and was compressed when the piston carried the breech block rearwards. Two marks were made. The earliest version (*117*), employed a simple cocking handle which travelled back and forwards on the right hand side with the bolt. The Mk 2 cocked like the BESA, ie the pistol grip slid forward and engaged the underside of the piston and drew it to the back when the grip was retracted.

The name BESAL led to identification difficulties when the BESA came along so it was renamed the Faulkoner. It shot well, and within the trials afforded gave every promise of being a practical weapon. Fortunately the Royal Small Arms Factory was never bombed and the need to make the BESAL never arose.

The BESA Machine Gun

In 1937 Vaclav Holek produced the Zb-53 Model 1937. This was similar in operating principles to the Zb 26 and in 7.92mm calibre. It was a tank gun with a heavy barrel and an unusual method of cocking in which the pistol grip was pushed forward and when pulled back withdrew the piston and the bolt to the rear. It was belt fed of very sturdy design incorporating a device to produce two alternative rates of fire of 450 and 750rpm.

The political situation was such that time was short. The British acquired manufacturing rights and the weapon was made at Enfield and by BSA at Birmingham in 7.92 calibre, necessitating the manufacture of a new round in Britain. The name BESA came from **B**rno, **E**nfield and **BSA**.

The gun was capable of prolonged bursts and was an excellent tank gun. Its only drawback, perhaps, was the need to lift the top cover plate to insert the belt and this required a clear space of 8in above the gun. Barrel changing also was not very simple.

When BSA started manufacturing they had to modify the gun for mass production and at this time they eliminated the variable rate of fire device.

The BESA was used throughout the war in British Tanks. It was, incidentally, used in its original form by the Germans when they occupied Czechoslovakia and took over the Brno factory.

After the war the 7.92mm round was discontinued and the American .30 calibre Browning used.

The BESA was also manufactured in 15mm calibre by BSA for armoured cars. Only 3 200 were made and they are now totally obsolete. Firing at 450 rounds a minute it was a very effective gun.

P.H.M.G.—F

Post war-Development
After World War II a very critical appraisal was carried out by the
"Ideal Calibre Committee" to decide on the calibre of the next
generation weapons. It was eventually decided in 1947 that the requirements for the Infantry sub-machine gun, rifle and machine gun could
all be met using a calibre of .280in (7mm). This would provide a light
effective rifle capable of firing fully automatic and a machine gun
capable of operating out to 1 800 metres. There was considered to be
no requirement for long range indirect fire.

The TADEN Machine Gun
Several different .280 calibre machine guns were produced in prototype, all based on the Zb system with various methods of actuating
the bolt feed. The most promising was the TADEN which obtained its
name from Lt Col Turpin and Enfield. This was a sustained fire gun,
tripod mounted with a quick change barrel system. It functioned well
and met the requirements for volume of fire, range, reliability and
accuracy but in 1952 it was decided that the .280 round would not be
adopted so no further work was done.

The X11E4 Machine Gun
When the 7.62mm round based on the Winchester .308 was standardised for NATO another machine gun was developed. This too was
based on the Zb—or Bren—principle with belt feed. The gun could
really be said to be a heavy barrel Bren adapted to produce a large
volume of fire. There was a high degree of co-operation between
Enfield and the School of Infantry and the gun was found to be very
accurate. It had however three drawbacks. The feed system was operated from the piston which was beneath the tilting bolt and a shaft was
brought up on the left of the gun which rotated as the piston reciprocated. At the top of the shaft it fitted into a feed arm which moved from
left to right as the shaft rotated one way and from right to left as the
shaft rotated back. With the gun lifting a long length of belt, as for
example firing over a wall, there were high frictional losses in the feed
system and the gun slowed down. Also the body was machined from
the solid which required a number of operations and was expensive to
produce. Lastly there were a number of projections on the body which
caught in undergrowth, personal equipment etc.
    In 1958 a series of comparative trials were held to determine the
best GPMG. The X11E4 was fired against the American M60, the
Belgium FN, MAG, the French AA52. the Swiss SIG and the Madsen-
Saetter MG. The trial was long and comprehensive and took into

account accuracy, reliability, low temperature and elevated temperature firings, and environmental tests of sand, mud and water. Eventually the FN MAG was considered to be the best all round gun and somewhat better than the X11E4.

As we have already seen, the FN guns are largely built around Browning's patents and John Browning's son Val and his son John continued the family connection. The MAG therefore is basically a machine gun developed from the locking system and operating method of the Browning Automatic Rifle. The BAR it will be recalled locked into the top of the body and the MAG uses the same system but locking on to shoulders below the action. The MAG is a sturdy gun well adapted for mass production and capable of firing any round with a base no larger than the 7.92mm Mauser merely by fitting the appropriate barrel. The feed mechanism is taken directly—as are those of many modern machine guns—from the German MG42 type (qv). The gun owes its success in coping with adverse conditions to its extremely powerful buffer which consists of a series of saucer shaped washers mounted in the butt. When the piston strikes the first of these it absorbs the energy by deforming into a flat plate and the successive washers do the same. When this strain energy is released the plates become saucers again and the surge of energy throws the recoiling parts forward with a velocity only slightly less than the rearward velocity they possessed on contact with the buffer. It should be noted that a fast firing gun like this (750–1 000rpm) has a "hard" buffer and no energy is lost. A slower firing gun like the Bren has a "soft" buffer designed to absorb the recoil energy and thus make the firer's task easier. The trigger mechanism also is a direct copy of the German MG 42.

Initially the L7A1 guns as they were known in Britain, were produced by FN at Herstal, Liège, but later they were manufactured at Enfield. The Director General of Artillery's department originally planned to have a light plain steel barrel for the Infantry Section gun and a heavy barrel with a Stellite liner for the sustained fire role. The Stellite liner is a non-ferrous alloy of Cobalt, Chromium, Tungsten and Molybdenum made by Laval et frères in Belgium and the Deloro Stellite Co, in UK. It is very hard, difficult to machine and has the great advantage of maintaining its strength at high temperatures. The original liners were made by the FN tool room and were very satisfactory but the production version had a lot of failures. These were eventually ascribed to inability to manufacture to the very close tolerances essential to produce a good interference fit. Eventually after a great deal of development and expenditure the idea of the heavy barrel was abandoned when success was in sight and it was decided to produce a conversion kit consisting of a tripod, dial sight and two spare light barrels all held at Company HQ, to convert any four guns to the sustained fire role.

The gun has now been in service for eight years. It has been very successful but there is a feeling that at 23½lb it is too heavy for the light role in jungle country and its sustained fire capability is in no way comparable with the water cooled Vickers it superseded.

The L8A1 Tank Machine Gun

The decision not to adopt the US M73 tank machine gun required the development of a new tank co-axial gun and the L7A1 Infantry gun was modified. To prevent fumes in the crew compartment the gas regulator system was re-designed from the original gun which exhausts its fumes to atmosphere and also a tube was added leading from the regulator to the muzzle so that any gas emerging is sucked forward. It should be noted that since the barrel goes out forward when it is changed, the whole gun must come back into the turret for changing barrels. With the demise of the Stellite liner a heavy plain steel barrel was developed for tank use. The feed is still from the left only and the empty cases are caught in a bag under the gun.

L37A1

This is the flexibly mounted tank gun and consists of the L8 gun but with sights and a butt.

L20A1

This is the helicopter gun and consists of a modified L7A2 with a heavy barrel.

Future Developments

At the time of writing the Americans have announced that their troops throughout the world including their NATO element in Europe will be armed with .223 (5.56mm) calibre rifles. Since it was at American insistence that the .280 round was abandoned for the 7.62mm round this is a complete volte face. This decision poses problems for all the NATO countries. FN in Belgium, Heckler and Koch in Germany and France, SIG in Switzerland and Beretta in Italy all have .223 rifles and are developing light machine guns in that calibre. Britain—which decided in 1959 to abandon all research and buy foreign—is placed in an awkward position. Although no decisions have been made and no policy yet adopted it seems that our next light machine gun will be of a type similar to the Stoner LMG and for sustained and vehicle fire we shall retain the 7.62mm L7A2 and L8A1 guns and accept two types of ammunition.

The ADEN Gun

In 1945 it became obvious that modern aircraft were so fast and the vital assemblies so well protected that the chances of successful engagement with 20mm guns was diminished. It was decided to produce a fast firing 30mm gun as armament for fighter aircraft. We took from the Germans the design of a 30mm revolver type weapon similar to their Mauser 213 gun. This was developed at Enfield and produced at the Royal Ordnance Factory at Nottingham with the name ADEN from **A**rmament **D**evelopment **EN**field.

The gun is gas operated on the revolver principle with a single barrel and 5 chambers. The gun fires at 1 200–1 400 rounds a minute. Two barrels and two types of ammunition were developed, one low velocity and the other high velocity. Subsequently the low velocity round was discontinued and the gun now uses only the high velocity round and barrel producing a muzzle velocity of 2 600ft/s.

Like a pistol revolver the Aden has a chamberless barrel behind which is mounted the five chambered breech cylinder. The loading of the round from the belt into the cylinder is accomplished in two stages; first it is rammed through the disintegrating link belt so that the nose enters the chamber, the chamber then rotates one further position and the round is rammed home and finally the chamber revolves in line with the barrel and the round is electrically fired. As the shell leaves the chamber it drives a steel sleeve into the barrel to ensure there is no gas escape between cylinder and barrel.

After firing, the breech cylinder and barrel recoil and are then returned to the runout position. Gas is tapped off from a vent into a gas cylinder and the piston is driven to the rear to operate two slides which feed, load and fire the gun.

The empty case is ejected as the slide comes forward again, after the rotation of the breech cylinder and feed sprockets, when a ramp on the front slide engages the ejector lever causing the ejector to flick the empty case to the rear.

With the development of air to air missiles the gun has been used on ground attack aircraft but modern thought seems now to be favouring guns once again for air to air battle.

The RARDEN Gun

The vast Russian bloc superiority in armour means that our tanks will be able to devote little effort to the enemy armoured personnel carriers, so a 30mm gun has been developed to be mounted in a proportion of our armoured personnel carriers to deal with this threat.

It is basically a large self loading rifle with a limited automatic capacity for anti aircraft work. The method of operation is known as long recoil. The barrel and breech block recoil for some 13in which is greater than the length of an unfired round. The barrel then runs out and when it is fully forward the next round is rammed home. As it enters the chamber the sliding breech block is released to come across and support it. The gun is clip loaded taking 6 rounds, and produces a muzzle velocity in excess of 3 6ooft/s with the Armour Piercing Discarding Sabot round and 3 25oft/s with the high explosive round. The long recoil was designed to reduce the forces on the mounting, and the rear loading and the sliding breech block give a short inboard length.

Not only is the gun going into the AFV 432 for Infantry use but also into the FOX range of reconnaissance and combat vehicles.

The name comes from **R**oyal **A**rmament **R**esearch and **D**evelopment Establishment and **En**field where it was designed and developed by a brilliant engineer named Brint. The H.E. round is Hispano-Suiza.

With this gun, of extreme accuracy and armour penetration, it is expected that the Infantry will destroy the enemy APC at ranges around 1000m where any troops who survive can be engaged by artillery and infantry mortars.

CLASSIFICATION OF VICKERS MACHINE GUNS
In British Service the changes to existing models were denoted by a * added to the current mark number and new models were given a new mark number.

.303in calibre
Machine Gun.   *Brief description*

Mk I Introduced by "List of Changes" No 16217 on Nov 26, 1912. The standard water cooled gun in Land Service. The last Regular units to be equipped with it were the Parachute Battalions who employed it in the Radfan.

Mk I* Introduced by L of C 22675 dated Feb 25, 1918 but it was in use before this date. The first Air Service gun, using a Mk I jacket with 3 sets of louvres cut to assist in air cooling. The front end cap was opened out and the steam tube removed. It was a synchronized gun weighing 27½lb.

Mk II Introduced by L of C 22675 with effect June 8, 1917. An air cooled aircraft gun with a smaller, perforated casing. It had no fused spring box. Weight 22lb.

Mk II* Introduced by L of C A3377 dated June 24, 1927. Similar to the Mk II, fitted with a cocking lever. Mk II* A was right hand feed. Mk II* B left hand feed. Weight 21lb.

Mk III An Air Service gun with a perforated barrel casing like the

Mk II and a muzzle attachment with flash hider which increased the overall length by 4 inches. Either left or right hand feed.

Mk IV Recorded in L of C A7771 of May 15, 1930. It was a prototype Armoured Fighting Vehicle gun, water cooled, similar in operation and cooling to the Mk I gun. Never in service.

Mk IV A Introduced by L of C A7771 and declared obsolescent. It was a factory modified Mk I gun, left or right hand feed, with a dovetail mounting plate for AFV use. Weight 38lb.

Mk IV B Introduced in L of C A7771. Factory modified Mk I gun with modified trunnion block and barrel casing for AFV use. Weight without water and shoulder piece 38lb. With water and shoulder piece 70lb.

Mk V Air Service gun similar to Mk III but with a side opening top cover.

Mk VI Introduced in L of C A9478 of Aug 17, 1934. Generally similar to the Mk IV B but a strengthened dovetail mounting. Left or right hand feed. Corrugated casing. Alloy fusee cover. Weight without water 41¾lb.

Mk VI* Introduced in L of C 3369 of Oct 26, 1938. Factory converted Mk I for AFV use with a trunnion block with an inlet and outlet connection for attachment to the tank cooling system. Left or right hand feed. Corrugated casing. Weight without water and shoulder piece 42¾lb.

Mk VII Improved Mk VI with a stronger dovetail mounting integral with the ejection sleeve, sweated and screwed into the trunnion block. Left or right hand feed. Thicker plain casing. Weight without water and shoulder piece 47¼lb.

The Mk I gun was declared obsolete in L of C w/1231 dated April 24, 1968. The Mks IV A, IV B, VI, VI* and Mk VII declared obsolete in L of C C2022 dated August 24, 1944.

.5in calibre

The .5in gun was basically a scaled up Mk I .303 gun with the following differences:

(a) Recoil operated but no muzzle assistance; (b) Fusee springs of the compression type; (c) The slides in the breech casings connected in one piece called the resistance piece; (d) No extension of the left barrel side plate and the feed operated by the barrel trunnion block and (e) Feed block and extractor modified for rimless ammunition.

Mk I Introduced by L of C A7772 of August 10, 1933. It was an experimental ground service model resembling the .303 Mk I gun without muzzle cup or attachment but having a conical flash hider. Rate of fire was reduced by a delay action pawl in the rear lever which held up the crank until the barrel was fully forward. A buffer spring absorbed the recoil of the barrel extension and accelerated it forward. Left and right hand feed. Ground sights and tripod fittings provided. Weight empty 52lb.

Mk II Introduced by L of C A7772 of Feb 5, 1932. The first AFV pattern. It had an offset pistol grip trigger, adjustable for single shot or automatic. Delay pawl and buffer spring as Mk I. Dovetailed mounting riveted below.

Mk III Naval Service modified from Mk I. Fitted ejector tube. No delay pawl and stronger buffer spring gave 700 rounds/minute. Automatic fire only with remote control. Pull type cocking lanyard provided. Water system similar to .303 Mk I but no condenser tube fitted. Fired disintegrating link belt.

Mk IV Introduced by L of C A9603 of Nov 6, 1933. Only a few were made. It had left and right hand feed and differed from the Mk II in having a narrower dovetail plate, and mounting base, to enable it to be interchanged with the .303in Mk IVA, IVB and VI in the No 8, 9, or 10 MG mounting. The ejector tube was in two parts; the rear part was riveted to the trunnion block with its front end coned to fit the forward part which was riveted to the mounting base and coned at the front end. Weight, bare, 58lb. Rate of fire 650–700rpm.

Mk V Introduced L of C A9603 of Nov 6, 1933. It differed from the Mk IV in having a detachable ejection tube and the bottom plates, side plates and trunnion block were of strengthened design. The Mks I, II, IV and V guns were declared obsolete by L of C C2022 of August 24, 1944.

The manufacturer denoted the class of weapon by a Class Letter. These were:

Class A An air cooled rifle calibre gun with an aluminium sleeve over the barrel. A finned muzzle cup. Fired from a rear sear. The body was continued forward to the muzzle on both sides of the barrel. It was a tank machine gun but not adopted for British Service.

Class B An air cooled .5in gun. No sleeve or jacket over the barrel. The body was continued forward on both sides of the barrel to the muzzle. Large flash hider. An aircraft gun used in British service.

Class C The standard water cooled .303 Mk I Vickers and adapted for the Mk I*.

Class D An air cooled rifle calibre aircraft gun. In British Service as the Vickers Mk II.

*Class D and Class D** A water cooled high velocity anti-aircraft machine gun of .5 calibre with a long barrel and firing a special high velocity round. In limited British service.

Class E A class D rifle calibre gun either belt or drum feed. Not in British service.

Class F Based on the class D rifle calibre gun drum fed only. Narrower diameter casing than the class D.

Class G An air cooled belt fed rifle calibre aircraft machine gun. Similar to the British Mk III gun. A narrower diameter perforated casing with a muzzle attachment but no flash hider.

Class J Air cooled aircraft machine gun of rifle calibre. Known as the Vickers Central Action Gun with a coil spring mounted internally behind the lock.

Class K An air cooled aircraft machine gun of rifle calibre. Known as the Vickers gas operated gun. In RAF service.

Class L An air cooled ground machine gun of rifle calibre known in British Service as the Vickers Berthier Light Machine gun.

The above list is not comprehensive and it is probable that there were class letters for the other .5 machine guns.

CHAPTER EIGHT

Czechoslovakian Machine Guns

IN 1922 the armament firm of Czeskoslovenska Zbrojovka Akciova Spolecnost v Brne of Brno was formed. It was a government majority holding company with shares held by Skoda and 5 per cent by the employees. Its first gun was the French Hotchkiss model 1922 manufactured under licence and in 1924 it built its first original design known when production got under way as the Zb 26. This gun was a great success. It was a gas operated, tilting block locking, magazine fed gun easily distinguished by the finned barrel and the gas cylinder reaching almost to the muzzle. This gun was the weapon from which the British Bren gun was derived.

The Zb company had a brilliant designer in Vaclav Holek who was ably supported by a very competent design team which included his brother Emanuel, Anton Marek, an Austrian by birth and a Pole named Antonin Podrabsky.

After the Zb 26 came the Zb 27 and Zb 30, all developments of the 26. The Zb 34 incorporated all the British modifications to the Zb 26 and in 7.92mm sold widely.

In 1937 Holek produced the model 53 which was manufactured in England and named the BESA. Similarly the Czech gun Zb-60 model 38 made in 15mm was made by BSA and called the BESA 15mm Mk. I.

All these guns were gas operated. Zb did produce one gun, the Zb 50 produced in 1932, recoil operated, which was the work of Anton Marek. This gun was very advanced. It introduced cocking by having two handles that were pushed forward and when retracted withdrew the bolt. This was later incorporated in the model 53 (BESA) in a single pistol grip. Another very unusual device was a holding open system that kept the bolt to the rear when the belt was exhausted. This is common on magazine fed guns but infrequently met on belt feeds. Another unique feature was the safety catch which when applied not only locked the sear but deflected the nose of the round down so that if the bolt did come forward the round was not chambered. The bolt was a tilting into lock type similar to the gas operated guns. After firing, as the barrel and bolt came back together they extended a spring which was attached to a claw type accelerator. When the bolt was ready for unlocking this spring came into play, pivoted the bolt out of its locking recess and hurled it rearwards. This spring operated accelerator is uncommon.

When the Germans marched into Czechoslovakia they took over the factory at Brno and kept the production line going and so basically the same LMG and tank machine guns were being used by both sides.

After the war the Russians had control of the country but unlike most of the satellites she had a lot of freedom to manufacture her own weapons and ammunition and was not forced to produce a Soviet designed gun.

In 1952 the factory produced the Vzor 52—model 52. It was obviously following the pre-war line of gas operated guns which followed the Zb 26 but it was chambered for the Czech 7.62mm intermediate cartridge known as the M52. This cartridge is not interchangeable with the current Russian M43 7.62mm intermediate round but is somewhat similar in shape, slightly larger and heavier and produces a higher muzzle velocity. The gun is noteworthy for several aspects. It can take either a 25 round top mounted magazine or a 100 round continuous link belt feeding from the left, without any alteration or additional fitting on the gun. The gas action is exactly the same as the Bren but the cocking system is that of the BESA. The belt feed mechanism is operated from the piston using a simple cam path and follower. It is very efficient and makes the arrangement used in the British X11E4 look very clumsy. The designer has gone to great lengths to make the entire mechanism dust and sand proof. With a magazine feed it fires at 900rpm which is fast for an infantry gun. With belt feed—presumably with an anti-aircraft role in mind—it fires at 1 200rpm. The gun uses pressings and lost wax castings and both design and method of manufacture are sophisticated. It is very accurate, easily controlled but susceptible to the ingress of dirt.

In 1956 the Czechs, under Russian pressure, gave up their M52 round and the gun was re-chambered for the Russian M43 round. The gun using the Russian ammunition is known as the Vz 52/57.

In 1959 a new General Purpose Machine Gun was produced. It is an interesting gun, being gas operated with a tilting block and incorporating the pistol grip to cock the gun. It has a light barrel for the LMG and a heavy barrel weighing $8\frac{1}{2}$lb for sustained fire. With the light barrel it fires at about 120 rounds a minute and with the heavy barrel 250 rounds a minute are claimed which it can sustain for 2min before the barrel must be changed. Probably the single most interesting fact is that the gun can be purchased to fire either the old Russian 1908 rimmed round of 7.62mm calibre or the rimless NATO 7.62mm round. It shows from this that the Russians are still using Czechoslovakia as a gateway to the West. There is also a Russian boat tailed heavy bullet available which with the dial sight allows indirect fire out to 5 000yd.

The gun weighs 20lb with the heavy barrel—which is 4lb lighter than the British GPMG.

It would appear that the change of political control has in no way prevented the Czech industry from producing fine weapons.

The next Czech project may well be a weapon system in which certain common parts, ie bolt, piston and body are added to selected barrels, feeds and trigger mechanisms to produce a whole family of weapons after the Stoner pattern. The vital question is what calibre will it employ? If it uses the M43 round it will not be an effective long range gun so perhaps we shall see a newly developed round for this project.

CHAPTER NINE

French Machine Guns

Hotchkiss Guns

BENJAMIN HOTCHKISS was an American born in Watertown, Connecticut in 1826. He helped design many of the famous Colt revolvers whilst working in Hartford. He had designs accepted by the US Government for barrel rifling and for a new percussion fuse.

In 1867 he went to France and a new metallic cartridge case he designed was manufactured at the Government Arsenal of St Etienne. In 1871 he produced a 5 barrel revolving cannon of 37mm calibre which was suitable for military use and also as an anti-torpedo boat gun. This, although similar at first sight, was quite different to the Gatling and more complex. The hand crank on the right of the gun controlled loading, firing, extracting and rotation by rotating a worm partly helical and partly circular. The helical portion rotated the barrels from one indexed position to the next whilst the circular portion locked the barrels at the indexed position for loading, firing and extraction simultaneously in different barrels. There were four versions of the 37mm gun and a 40mm for fortifications, a 47mm for naval use and a naval 57mm. The 37mm gun weighed 1 200lb and was 6ft long.

In 1884 Hotchkiss amalgamated with William Armstrong and the gun was manufactured at Elswick. In 1885 Hotchkiss died and in 1887 another American, Lawrence V. Benét became Chief Engineer. He was the son of General Benét, Chief of Ordnance USA Army, who, it will be recalled, designed the new round for Gatling. In 1892 Benét purchased from Captain Baron Adolf von Odkolek, an Austrian nobleman, the patents of his machine gun, which incorporated the first gas piston in a cylinder under the barrel. The prototype was tested in 1895 and it worked well but overheated badly. Benét increased the mass of metal around the chamber and increased the cooling area tenfold by adding five doughnut shaped brass fins which formed a ready recognition feature. The gun was a 8mm gas operated weapon with a bolt locking action, similar in principle to the Navy Lee 6mm straight pull rifle, but here a lug was forced up out of the bolt to engage in the body. The feed system was a sprocket drawing a strip through from the right. The rounds were held on top of the strip. This gun was used by the Japanese in their war against Russia in 1904–5.

The Benét-Mercié Machine Gun

Mercié was originally a French workman who impressed Benét with his skill and intelligence. Together they produced a gun which was adopted by the American army in 1909 in .30–06 calibre. It locked by means of a "fermature nut" which locked the barrel to the breech block by rotating over them both when the gas piston caused it to revolve. The ammunition was placed below the clip. It was adopted by the USA and the story is told that when the Mexican partisan Pancho Villa raided Columbus, New Mexico, one night in 1916, the defenders who were armed with the Benét-Mercié did not fire a shot. They emphasized afterwards that it was too difficult to load at night! The Colt and Springfield armouries made some 670 of these guns which were some used for training purposes.

The Hotchkiss Model 1914

War in 1914 found the French unready. The arsenals at St Etienne and Chatellerault could not produce enough guns and Hotchkiss and Co were called upon to provide as many machine guns as possible. The 8mm Hotchkiss machine gun was by now well tried and was further improved. This 1914 model was a great success. Lt Col Chinn in "The Machine Gun" records how two guns dug in 140yd behind the crest in a position near Hill 304 fired for 10 days and nights in June 1916 during the defence of Verdun. Each gun fired over 75 000 rounds without failure.

The American Army was equipped with this gun when it entered the war in 1917. It managed to have the gun re-chambered for the .30–06 round and used the gun until the end of the war.

The St Etienne Machine Gun

This was produced by the arsenal of that name in 1907. It was a complicated gun, unreliable and "gimmicky". Instead of the gas piston being forced back to unlock the bolt and carry it rearwards, the piston is driven forward. The piston is attached to a spring loaded rod and a rack. The rack runs out across a spur gear wheel which rotates a lever the end of which is in a cam slot in the bolt. The spring drives the piston back and the reversing gear drives the bolt forward. This gun was used by the French Army who replaced it as quickly as possible with the Hotchkiss Model 1914.

The Chauchat Machine Gun

This gun was so called after the Colonel of that name who was Chairman of the Commission recommending its adoption by the French Army. It was the only French machine gun until current times that was not gas operated. It was a long recoil operated gun with the barrel and bolt locked together during a recoil distance in excess of the length of an unfired round. The bolt was then unlocked and held to the rear holding the empty case whilst the barrel ran forward. A spring loaded ejector pushed the case out of the right hand side of the body, and the barrel then released the bolt which fed and chambered the round. Whilst the bolt was feeding the round the bolt head was prevented from rotating by a conical cotter which came through the bolt body. As soon as the round was chambered the cotter rode under a recess in the gun body and the bolt body rotated the head to lock it to the barrel.

The French 8mm round had a very large base and so the magazine was semi-circular. The American .30 had a smaller base and so the magazine was only slightly curved.

All things considered the Chauchat was probably one of the crudest, most unreliable and cheaply made guns ever to come into service. Nine American Divisions were armed with the Chauchat and probably 50 per cent of the guns were thrown away as useless. The American Army Department purchased 37 864 Chauchats between December 1917 to April 3, 1918. They were all made and inspected by the French and the contract bound the Americans to accept them once they had passed inspection. Not a very good example of American business acumen!

The Chatelleraut Machine Gun
After World War I it was essential to the French that the Chauchat be replaced by a weapon properly designed and constructed. In 1921 the prototype of a gun, named after the arsenal at Chatelleraut, was produced, and with it a new 7.5mm round copied from the Swiss. In design it was extremely similar to the Browning Automatic Rifle using a locking system embodying exactly the same principle. The French advertised the gun as being available for sale before it was properly developed and in 1926 a Rumanian delegation firing the gun had a bore explosion which severely injured the firer and some of the watching commission.

Similar explosions took place when the gun entered French service and very quickly it got a bad reputation with troops which was not abated by the glowing press reports of the time. When improved it was known as the Model 24/29.

The 1924/29 Model was magazine fed from the top and the 1931 model was for Tank, Armoured Car or Fortress use. The vehicle gun had a drum like the Lewis mounted vertically on the right hand side. The Fortress version could not only take the magazine on either side but also had an arrangement by which water was injected by the bolt into the chamber and barrel after the spent case was extracted. The next version was the Model 1934/39 belt fed for aircraft use.

The Model 24/29 had the unusual feature of two triggers—the rear one giving automatic fire, the front one having a disconnector for single shot.

The 24/29 was the main French LMG in 1940. It was used against the Germans in their offensive and the French Forces in North Africa who, under Admiral Darlan, opposed the Allies, also used it. The French wars in Indo-China and Algiers saw the last large scale use of this gun.

The AA 52

After World War II the French Army had no modern weapons of native design. The machine guns in use were the British supplied Vickers and Bren guns, the USA M1919 A4 Browning and a large number of German MG 42s. These weapons were used in Indo-China and the problem of the diversity of ammunition and the difficulty in getting spare parts to the right unit at the right time contributed materially to the unhappy sequence of events culminating at the disaster of Dien Bien Phu.

The AA 52 was designed with the cardinal French policy requirement of cheapness very much in the forefront. The full name is the "Arme Automatique Transformable Model 1952" which can be freely translated to mean the General Purpose Machine Gun Model 52.

The French have always—with one exception in the past—produced gas operated guns. In the AA 52 they have gone to the principle of blowback operation and as this is the first such gun to be described here, it will be covered rather more fully.

The basic principle of blowback is extremely simple. It is the utilisation of the gas pressure to force the cartridge case backwards out of the chamber, driving the breech block or bolt back against a return spring to carry out the cycle of operations. When a parallel sided round—such as the 9mm Parabellum—is so used to operate a sub machine gun there are few problems. The pressure is low—10tonf/in^2—and the parallel sides of the case provide obturation and prevent the gas escaping back through the breech whilst the case is moving rearwards. When however the cartridge used is a full power rifle round the situation is very different. The pressure is about 22tonf/in^2 and the case is tapered. When the gas pressure is produced it forces the case hard against the chamber walls and prevents the case moving and at the same time it pushes the base of the cartridge back and so stretches the case. When the peak pressure is passed the chamber walls return to their original size and so does a well designed cartridge case but if the pressure has been too high the case will be permanently expanded. The effect of this is to cause the case to rupture its weakest section which is just across the shoulder and the case goes back leaving the neck in the chamber. If the cartridge is lubricated or the chamber fluted the case may go back too rapidly with the result that it is unsupported as it emerges from the chamber and bursts.

Thus the essence of a successful blowback system is to hold the case in the chamber without movement until the pressure is well past its peak and then allow the residual pressure to drive the case and bolt back. If a low powered round is used the mass and resulting inertia of a heavy breech block will be sufficient for this but when employing a high powered round some positive delaying device is essential. In the AA this delay is achieved by using a breech block in two parts which for simplicity I will call the bolt head and bolt body (see page 28). The bolt head carries a lever with a short arm projecting out into a recess in the body of the gun at the moment of firing and the long arm of the lever rests on the bolt body. As the bolt head starts to move back the lever starts to rotate. There is a mechanical disadvantage due to the difference in length of the lever arms and the bolt body is accelerated backwards and the bolt head moves slowly thus supporting the cartridge case. When the lever has rotated out of the body of the gun the whole breech block travels rearwards with its two parts separated by the length of the long lever arm. The return spring drives the bolt back, the bolt head chambers the round and stops but the bolt body closes up and causes the lever to rotate again into the gun body. As the two parts of the bolt come together the firing pin is driven forward into the cap.

The gun itself is cheaply made utilising running welds to join two semi-cyclinders. In short it is a cheap gun—using a monopod under the body with a bipod forward instead of the usual tripod. The gun appears to work on the very limit of safety as the photograph (*167*) shows.

The AA 52 was employed in Algeria. Initially it was issued only to Parachute Regiment of the Foreign Legion but eventually it was held by most infantry units.

CHAPTER TEN

German Machine Guns

GERMANY started World War I with 12 500 Maxim machine guns in the hands of troops and 50 000 more on order. These were being made by Deutsche Waffen und Munitionsfabriken in Berlin. They produced the heavy, water cooled Maxim known as the '08 pattern, sledge mounted initially, which remained the principle German Infantry machine gun throughout that war. It weighed 41lb and was really too heavy for mobile operations. A lighter version was produced with a shoulder stock and a 50 round belt container on the right hand side and a bipod. This was water cooled but with no circulating system or condensers and weighed 31 pounds without water. It was known as the '08/15.

The Maxim was mounted on the top of the Zeppelins for air defence but when aircraft became faster and started to be used for aerial combat the Maxim was considered to be somewhat heavy and Karl Heinemann of DWM re-designed the gun, broke the toggle upwards like the Vickers and improved the feed arrangements. His gun, called the Parabellum, weighed only 22lb and fired at 700 rounds a minute. It became the standard German forward firing aircraft gun and when Fokker produced his synchronising gear enabling it to fire through the airscrew the German Fokker aircraft were armed with it. The success of the German pilots can be judged by their victories. In April 1917, "Bloody April", the Royal Flying Corps lost 316 pilots and observers which was one third of their effective flying strength.

In 1916 the German engineer, Carl Gast, produced a novel gun which if developed at once could have had a tremendous influence on the fighting in the air. This was a recoil operated double barrelled gun fed from circular magazines mounted vertically on each side. The idea was that as a barrel and breech recoiled it furnished the energy to lock and fire the other which in turn gave energy to load, lock, fire, extract and eject the next round from the first barrel. Eventually the gun produced 1 800 rounds a minute. Each magazine held 180 rounds and could be changed in the air very quickly. If a stoppage occurred in one barrel the other could still fire single shots.

Late in the day the Germans gave this gun complete priority but the war ended before substantial numbers were delivered. After the war, story has it, the Germans tried to conceal from the Allied Commission the location of the manufacturing plant. Samples were sent to America for evaluation but with disarmament taking place nothing was done to develop the Gast further.

After the Versailles treaty the small arms manufacturing capacity of Germany was limited to those weapons made by the firm of Rheinmetall, which before the war had been second only to Krupps in volume of arms output, for the German Army. Due to the small size of the army Rheinmetall was unable to expand in Germany so it acquired control of the Solothurn Company in Switzerland as an outlet for its production. In 1929 Solothurn offered a light air cooled machine gun designed by Louis Stange, operated by short recoil and of ingenious if somewhat complicated design. This was followed by the improved MG 30. In 1932 Rheinmetall produced an air cooled aircraft gun—the MG 15 which fired from an open bolt. To make it suitable for synchronisation it was made to operate from a closed bolt and re-named the MG 17.

In 1936 Rheinmetall amalgamated with Borsig forming the most famous name in German small arms production. The first product was the MG 131, an aircraft gun of 13mm calibre with a MV of 2560ft/s, electrically fired and weighing only 40lb.

When Hitler came into power and flagrantly defied the French and British by re-arming, he encouraged the great arms firm of Mauser to re-start making machine guns. Their first venture was the MG 34.

The MG 34

This was the first General Purpose Machine Gun. It weighed 26lb which was light enough to enable it to be carried in the Infantry section, it was belt fed and when mounted on a tripod it could produce accurate sustained fire. Its rate of fire of 800–900rpm made it suitable for AA work and it was later slightly modified to become the standard tank gun throughout World War II. It was operated by short recoil and like nearly all short recoil guns of rifle calibre (including the Brownings and Vickers) it obtained additional power by using the expansion of the gases at the muzzle to operate a recoil intensifier—or muzzle booster—which accelerated the barrel backwards.

The bolt had a rotating head with an interrupted thread which locked into the barrel extension after being rotated by two cams which contacted rollers on the bolt head. After firing, the barrel and bolt recoiled together for three-sixteenths of an inch and the rollers on the bolt head were rotated by cam surfaces in the body. This freed the buttress thread whilst the chamber pressure was quite high so there was an element of blowback action to accelerate the bolt rearwards which was added to by the thrust surfaces between the bolt head and body.

The trigger provided single shot from pressure on the top half and full auto if the bottom segment was squeezed. The MG 34 was beautifully made but with excessively close tolerances which did not permit the ingress of dirt and sand and consequently under adverse conditions performance suffered.

The normal continuous link belts of 50 rounds were easily joined together for sustained fire whilst during Infantry movement a single belt could be carried in a metal drum on the left side of the gun. Some guns had a special feed cover which allowed the fitting of a double-drum spring operated saddle magazine which contained 75 rounds. When this was fitted the energy to operate the feed system came from the magazine springs and so the task of the gun was lightened. This produced an increased rate of fire which made it very suitable for AA mounting.

Throughout the war front line units were equipped with the MG 34. It was never completely replaced and at the height of the Russian campaign it was being manufactured by Mauser and Suhl in Germany, Steyr-Daimler-Puch in Austria, Brno in Czechoslovakia and a number of component manufacturers.

After the war large numbers of guns were sold and many found their way to Israel where they were used in the 1948 war, 1956 war and finally in the six-day war in 1967.

Probably more MG 34s were used in action than any other gun during World War II.

The MG 42

The MG 34 did not lend itself to the scale of production required to equip the vast German armies when they were fighting the British Commonwealth, Russia and America and in spite of all the captured Czech, Austrian, French and Italian guns, a new machine gun designed specifically for quantity production was produced. This was the MG 42. The body of the gun was designed for stamping and pressing processes with welding and riveting fabrication. The final shape of the design was determined by Dr Grunow of the Johannes Grossfuss concern who was an authority on metal-stamping design and production methods. The unique locking system was based on a patent taken out by Edward Stecke of Warsaw. The bolt head carries two rollers. Each roller is shaped like the wheel of a wheelbarrow with a thick centre section and a smaller diameter spindle projecting on each side. When the bolt head is going forward the rollers are held in to the centre but as soon as the bolt head enters the barrel extension they are forced out by cam paths. The thick centre section of the roller is in the bolt head but the projecting spindles are engaged in the grooves in the barrel extension and so the bolt head is firmly locked to the barrel. Until the rollers are forced out the firing anvil with its pin cannot move between them to reach the cap and so locking must be completed before firing can occur. After firing, the barrel and breech recoil together, assisted by a recoil intensifier at the muzzle, for $\frac{1}{4}$in until the centre portions of the rollers hit a cam path in the body of the gun which forces them inwards and unlocks bolt from barrel. The bolt is accelerated rearwards and the barrel is forced forward by its own return spring.

The feed system has been extensively copied by other gun designers. On the top of the bolt is a roller which engages in a curved feed arm mounted in the top cover plate. As the bolt reciprocates the forward end of the feed arm is moved from side to side and pawls attached to a pivoted arm alternately slide over the belt and pull it up. Since the arm moves both on the recoil stroke and the feed stroke of the bolt the belt is moved half a pitch each time which reduces the acceleration forces and smooths the feed. The British GPMG, the Swiss GPMG and the American M60 feeds are all based on the original MG 42. The trigger mechanism providing only automatic fire has a device controlling the moment at which the sear rises to ensure the meeting of the full face of the sear with that of the bent to prevent chipping of the meeting surfaces. This feature has also been widely copied.

The gun weighs 25lb with its bipod, fires at 1 200 rounds a minute from a continuous link belt and using the 7.92mm Mauser cartridge with a muzzle velocity of 2 575ft/s the heavy bullet (198 grains) is effective from a tripod out to 3 830yds.

The first known instance of its use in action is by Rommel's Panzer Grenadiers in May–June 1942 against the 8th Army's Gazala-Bir Hackeim positions.

In his book *The Machine Gun* Lt Col Chinn states that captured MG 42s were sent back to the United States from North Africa for examination. The Ordnance Department believed it to have so many good features that a contract was issued to the Saginaw Steering Gear Division of General Motors Corporation to develop two models of the MG 42, to be called the T24 machine gun, and full drawings. The drawings were completed in June 1943 and after various corrections the first gun was ready for firing on October 1, 1943. The gun was totally unsatisfactory and efforts were made to improve it until February 1944 when it was fired at the Aberdeen Proving Ground. The test was designated as "10 000 rounds endurance". After 1 483 rounds had been fired with 50 malfunctions, the test was suspended and the two guns sent to the Machine Guns Branch of the Small Arms Development Division. It was there found that the body of the gun had been made $\frac{1}{4}$in too short, the bolt had been so designed that it did not recoil far enough to clear the ejection opening, and the cocking handle had been made too short and interfered with the bolt during the recoil stroke. It was decided that the extensive re-design necessary to correct these serious defects in both body and bolt were not then worthwhile. The two models of the American made failure, the "Machine Gun Cal .30 T24" were sent to the Springfield Armoury and placed in its museum for reference and historical purposes. The contract for the work is stated to be $25 400.*

After the war the captured stocks of MG 42s were—unlike the MG 34 —not sold but retained by the various countries occupied by the Germans. The French initially re-equipped their armies with this gun, the Yugoslavs still have it as the Sarac.

The West German army adopted the MG 42 rechambered for the NATO 7.62mm cartridge in 1959. The gun was then called the MG 42/59. Production was re-started by Rheinmetall-Borsig and the gun is now known as the MG 3. The gun is basically unchanged with the exception of the insertion within the bolt body of a spring loaded plunger which when inserted one way up bears on the locking rollers and slows down the rate of fire from 1 200rpm to 600rpm. The plunger can easily be reversed to allow the full rate of fire.

There can be no doubt that the MG 42 has been the most successful GPMG yet designed. Even allowing for national pride the German re-adoption of the gun when they rebuilt their army is very significant.

The FG 42

The German Army was the first to use parachutists in war although the organisation of their forces was such that the airborne troops came under the Luftwaffe. Paratroops generally suffer from a lack of artillery and mortar support in the vital initial stages before heavy elements arrive to support them and therefore a rifle that can be used as a light machine gun offers obvious attractions.

When the German Airborne Forces invaded Crete they were largely armed with the Schmeisser MP 40—a sub machine gun of limited range. The British and New Zealand troops they encountered were equipped with rifles which outranged the German weapons.

As a result it was decided to press for a rifle that could be used in the assault at full auto and also be employed firing from a bipod as a LMG.

The weapon procurement department of the Luftwaffe, LC-6, had already produced and circulated a specification for such a weapon and two firms Rheinmetall and Krieghoff had prepared prototypes. The Rheinmetall design is ascribed to Louis Stange, Chief Designer of the

*International Armament, Vol. II, page 369

factory at Soemmerda, in Thuringia, and this was selected and named the Fallschirmjager Gewehr 1942—parachute rifle 1942. The army, which was developing the MP 43 did not approve of the weapon and it is said that chrome steel and managanese steel were deliberately diverted away. Rheinmetall either had no spare capacity or did not wish to antagonise the army so production was sub-contracted to Krieghoff.

By the time the weapon was ready the German parachutists were fighting defensive battles as ground troops. The FG 42 was used in the defence of Rhodes and later it was seen in quantity in the German parachutists' defence of Cassino.

The cartridge chosen was the powerful 7.92mm $\times$ 57 which was the standard round used by the '98 pattern Mauser rifle and the MGs 34 and 42. For airborne use the weapon was made with the minimum practical length of barrel. To counteract the violent recoil and blinding flash this produced, a combined muzzle brake and flash eliminator was fitted.

For rifle accuracy closed bolt firing was adopted but as a light machine gun the cooling advantages of open breech operation were required. A swivelling sear was provided which swung across the gun and engaged a bent at the back of the bolt when single shot was wanted and a bent at the front for automatic fire. The bolt was a close copy of that used on the Lewis gun and rotated under the drive of the piston post. After locking was completed there was still 1in for the fixed firing pin on the piston post to go forward to strike the cap and so with single shot selected the piston travelled 1in after trigger operation. It can readily be seen that with the bolt closed and the piston 1in from its fully forward position, the return spring was very nearly fully extended and there was no energy to propel the piston forward. A separate spring was therefore placed inside the bolt to provide the energy for single shot firing. When the Americans copied the FG 42 bolt for the M60 they even incorporated this spring which serves no purpose in a fully automatic machine gun.

Only about 6 000 FG 42s were made. The design had no new features but had a very interesting and unusual arrangement of proven ideas. It was probably the first genuine effort to provide a light weight machine gun with rifle accuracy at single shot.

Heckler and Koch

After 1945 the Mauser plant at Oberndorf was dismantled by the French and the work force dispersed. When Germany became a partner in the NATO organisation, the firm of Heckler and Koch took over the plant. They produced the HKG3 rifle for the army based on the CETME rifle designed in Spain by Mauser engineers. This is a delayed blowback rifle using a two part bolt with rollers in the bolt head engaging in recesses in the barrel extension which are forced in on firing and delay the backward movement of the breech face. This design was used by Heckler and Koch in a light machine gun. The gun is produced in .223in calibre (5.56mm) and also in limited numbers in the Russian 7.62 × 39 M43 intermediate round. In .223 it is called the HK 13, magazine fed and HK 23, belt fed. In 7.62mm × 39 it has the designation HK 12 when magazine fed and HK 22 when belt fed.

The HK 13 has recently been tested in this country. Using a special heavy barrel which can be changed quickly when heated, it has proved itself to be very reliable. It has operated particularly well under adverse conditions.

CHAPTER ELEVEN

Italian Machine Guns

THE STUDY of Italian machine guns is rendered somewhat complex by the fact that the manufacturing companies of Breda and Fiat made not only their own weapons and each others', but also made, sometimes jointly, weapons designed by independent companies. In 1930 Breda took over the Fiat arms plant. The tabulated data section at the rear of the book gives the Italian guns by manufacturer and in chronological order.

During the period at the end of the 19th century when Maxim's guns were taking over from Gatlings, Nordenfelts and Gardners, the Italians seem to have been living in something of a backwater.

Fiat Machine Gun
In 1901 Captain Giusseppe Perino of the Rome Artillery Factory designed a machine gun. Unlike the very great majority of sustained fire guns it was not belt fed but strip loaded from a magazine holding five strips each of 25 6.5mm rounds. The bottom strip was fed through the gun from left to right and the empty cases were replaced in the strip. As soon as one strip was emptied it fell out of the gun and the next one was forced across from the bottom of the magazine into the gun and the No 2 of the gun replenished the magazine by placing a loaded clip on top of those already in place. The gun was water cooled, weighed 50lb and was recoil operated with assistance from the muzzle booster. One unusual feature of the arm was that it had no bolt return spring. When the barrel was driven forward to the run out position by its own spring a lever, engaged in the bolt, was pivoted and the bolt flung forward. The gun was fired in competition with the Maxim in 1908 and the result encouraged the Italians to believe that they had a fine weapon. Development was continued and the 7.7mm cartridge was adopted in the 1908 model. In 1910 it was further improved and an air cooled version was tried. Finally after 14 years of effort the War came and as no preparation had been made to mass produce the gun it was abandoned and the Maxim—regarded as an interim measure whilst the Perino was refined—manufactured in quantity. This could have been a good gun but as always, the quest for perfection prevented the adoption of the adequate.

In 1908 Bethel Revelli, a native of Rome, designed a water cooled, delayed blowback operated machine gun weighing 38lb. This too had an unusual feed system utilising a metal container with 10 compartments each holding 5 rounds. The 5 rounds nearest the gun were fired, from the bottom in succession, and then the whole magazine moved over one compartment into the gun, and the firing of the next five was succeeded by another movement across. The rounds were lubricated before feeding. After firing the barrel recoiled with the block for half an inch and was then halted. A swinging wedge which held the barrel and block together was rotated out of engagement and the residual gas pressure forced the block back.

The Fiat concern manufactured the gun so it is called the Fiat Revelli. It was tested in America in 1911 but referred back for further development. During World War I Fiat produced many thousands of this model.

Fiat converted the water cooled Revelli into an air cooled aircraft gun, increased the cartridge lubrication to put up the rate of fire and it was used until Vickers and Lewis guns became available.

The 1926 Fiat Revelli was a light machine gun using once again a delayed blow back system. The magazine was pivoted on the side of the body and filled from a horse-shoe container. The magazine had no lips but the rounds were held in by a spring catch. When loaded the magazine was swung out at right angles to the gun and secured. If for any reason it was moved back to its parked position half a dozen rounds fell out on the ground. Again the ammunition was lubricated from a reservoir in the top of the cover. 2 000 of these guns were made by Fiat at Turin in an armament plant established there.

The Fiat 1928 gun retained the feed method of the 1926 version but abandoned Revelli's delayed blow back system in favour of recoil operation and used a locking system invented by Giuseppe Mascarucci who worked for a Fiat subsidiary called Safat. This was a hook mounted behind the barrel over the block and locking the two parts by dropping into a recess in the top of the bolt. (Note the similarity in principle to Maxim's Original model.) When the barrel recoiled the hook was lifted up, after a short period of free movement, and the bolt freed. Lubrication was no longer required for the ammunition since positive locking and correct head space prevented ruptured cases. The gun weighed 21lb, was air cooled but again no large order was placed.

Fiat used this operating principle in the 1928 aircraft gun, using a disintegrating link belt, with a muzzle booster to push the rate of fire up to 800 rounds a minute.

In 1935 Fiat reverted to Revelli's delayed blow back system with lubricated cases once again. Later models of this weapon employed a fluted chamber—probably the first to do so. The idea of the flutes was to allow gas to surround the case thus providing a cushion which, like oil, would prevent adhesion to the chamber walls. In this instance the idea did not function satisfactorily because the gun fired at only 120 rounds a minute. (Many modern delayed blow back rifles such as the German G3 and machine guns, as for example the French AA-52, now employ fluted chambers with success.)

Breda Machine Gun

The Breda concern was originally a locomotive works which came into armament manufacturing during World War I. The Fiat firm sub-contracted manufacture of the 1914 Model Revelli and supplied drawings for this purpose.

After the cessation of hostilities Breda stayed in armament work and in 1924 they produced a light machine gun. The pivoting magazine was used and the ammunition was lubricated. The bolt was locked to the barrel by a large nut which encircled both the bolt head and the rear of the barrel. When the block recoiled it pulled the nut and barrel back for about ⅜in. A lug on top of the nut struck a sloping plate which caused the nut to rotate and the bolt was freed to be blown back by the residual pressure. The gun in 6.5mm calibre weighed 20lbs and had a cyclic rate of 500 rounds a minute. It was fired in competition with the Fiat Model 1926 and Breda also got an order for 2 000 guns. The 1930 Breda model was basically the same gun as the 1924 type and was made in 6.5mm for native use and 7.92mm for export. The Italian Forces in the Desert Campaign were armed with this gun in 6.5mm. The barrel recoiled through a very poorly designed front bearing and as a result there was a very loose fit resulting in a widely dispersed cone of fire.

In the autumn of 1930 Breda took over Fiat's arms interests and with them the Safat Company. Safat designed an aircraft machine gun, shortly after the take-over, in 7.7mm (.303in). This weighed 27lb, fired at 800 rounds a minute and incorporated the Mascarucci lock. It used a fluted chamber with success and the calibre chosen allowed it to fire British ammunition acquired for the Vickers and Lewis guns. Guns were also made in 7.92mm for export. This gun, the Breda-Safat model 1935, was recoil operated with a gas-booster at the muzzle and became the standard Italian aircraft gun.

In 1937 Breda introduced an 8mm gas operated gun—their first so activated. It had a 20 round strip feed with the empty cases being replaced in the strip, and was locked by a sliding lug forced upwards by ramps on the piston. In spite of the gas operation, the lack of close tolerances in manufacture and the resulting inability to control the cartridge head space made the use of lubricated cases essential. The heavy barrel allowed a reasonable volume of fire and this led to its use on a tripod as a medium machine gun.

The 1938 model eliminated the strip feed and used a slightly curved box magazine mounted on top of the body and replaced the spade grips of the '37 with a pistol grip, but otherwise was the same.

Scotti Machine Guns

Alfredo Scotti was a designer from Brescia. He was not connected with any one firm but his designs were manufactured by Isotta-Fraschini, Grandi of Milan and Ansaldo amongst others. His guns were nearly all based on the idea of gas to unlock the bolt and blowback to carry out the remainder of the cycle. He produced a 7.7mm aircraft machine gun in 1928 and another in 12.7mm was among his more successful guns. His 20mm cannon was used by the Italian air force in World War II.

Post-war Development

After the 1939–45 war the Italians manufactured the German MG 42/59 under licence and for some years this has been their standard infantry gun.

The well known firm of Beretta who specialised in pistols and sub-machine guns before the war, introduced a new light machine gun in 1969. It is of .223 calibre (5.56mm) firing the Stoner developed Remington cartridge. It is an attractive gun, gas operated, weighing 12½lb and with a quick barrel change allowing 60–80 rounds a minute for a considerable period. It has not been adopted, at the time of writing, by the Italian armed forces.

CHAPTER TWELVE

Japanese Machine Guns

THE JAPANESE became aware of the potentialities of the Infantry machine gun very early on and in the early 1900s they manufactured the French Hotchkiss model 1897 under licence in Tokyo.

During the Russian-Japanese war of 1904–05 the Hotchkiss gun gave very good service and was also handled well by the Japanese Infantry.

The Japanese furnished their troops before Port Arthur with 72 Hotchkiss guns, allotted on the scale of 24 to each division, each group being under the immediate command of the divisional commander. They proceeded at once to exploit the gun as an attack weapon, dragged by hand, and thrown with the utmost boldness into the fight; and the evolution of the tactical handling of the new arm was speedily developed, and the importance of enfilade and overhead fire became paramount in the Japanese calculations.*

Illustrations of the successful tactical employment of guns by the Japanese are many. Captain von Beckmann, a German Military Attaché, reported: "At Mukden on March 1 all the machine guns of a whole Japanese division (12 to 18 guns) were brought into action upon a Russian point d'appui. The Russian fire was silenced, but burst out again whenever the machine gun fire slackened. The Japanese infantry used these pauses in the enemy's fire to press forward to close range under cover of their machine gun fire".

The history of the Russo-Japanese War has many instances of assaults brilliantly and successfully executed by the Japanese as the result of the skilful use of machine guns with overhead fire. On March 13, during the great battle of Mukden, the Japanese infantry were able to cross the river Fan, supported by machine gun fire at 1 800yd range, which, while the attack climbed from the river-bed and completed the difficult and arduous uphill assault, kept up their fire until the infantry were within 40yd of the Russian trenches. In a lecture on March 5, 1905, after the Ma-chun-tan action, the officer commanding the machine guns of the 2nd Japanese Division said: "I got a good position for the guns and, firing over the infantry's heads, covered their advance at a range of 1 200 yards. The enemy in their trenches fired heavily; but we were soon able to make them keep their heads down. Whenever I

* The Book of the Machine Gun by Langstaffe and Atteridge 1917

ceased fire up went their heads again. Each machine gun expended
1 500 rounds during the action which lasted about an hour".*

As a result of their successful employment of the Hotchkiss gun the
Japanese made extensive use of the gun in succeeding generations of
weapons.

Their medium machine gun was adopted in 1914 directly from the
Hotchkiss 1914 Model. The French gun was chambered for the 8mm
Lebel cartridge but the Japanese used the 6.5mm semi-rimmed bottle
necked cartridge known as the type 38. Because of the near parallel
sides of the case, the poor primary extraction and the inability of the
Japanese to control the cartridge head space by working to close
tolerances, it was necessary to lubricate the rounds before chambering.
This enabled the case to slide back freely and seat against the breech
face as soon as pressure developed in the cartridge.

The modifications to the French design were carried out by Lt
General Kijiro Nambu. He had previously designed the Japanese pistol
of that name but his modification to the Hotchkiss did not alter its
basic design in any way. The modified French Gun became the Type 3
and entered Japanese service in 1914. Amongst the detailed alterations
he carried out was the replacement of the ejector system by the very
effective pivoting ejector used in the Lewis gun.

The next gun produced by Nambu was the Taisho (model) 11 which
came out in 1922. This had the characteristic finned barrel, which had
been put on the smooth contoured French '14 model in the Type 3,
and was used in virtually all Japanese machine guns. It is doubtful
if finning is of any great assistance in improving heat transfer from the
barrel to the surrounding air. It does increase the cooling area but at a
cost of increased weight and the gaps between the fins harbour dirt
and oil which burn off to produce a heat haze which makes sighting
difficult. If the machine gun is moving through the air—as in a tank
gun—then the fins are worthwhile but not in the ground role.

The Type 11, 1922, introduced a new feed system, still employing
the 6.5mm round. A hopper was placed on the left-hand side of the body.
Six five-round infantry rifle chargers went in and were held down by a
heavy spring loaded arm. The bottom of the hopper had a sliding ratchet
which on the backward movement of the bolt pulled the bottom rounds
towards the bore. The clip was held. On the forward stroke a round was
fired. When the bottom five rounds were fired the clip was ejected and
the spring forced the remaining rounds down. Thus the total capacity
of 30 rounds could be expended. Although this system enabled the rifle
men to feed the machine gun it had several disadvantages. The hopper

---

Machine Guns by Lt Col G. S. Hutchinson

disturbed the balance of the gun which although not important when fired from a bipod made handling awkward and firing on the move difficult. It also collected dirt and dust which collected on the rounds and since the rounds were lubricated made a grinding paste in the chamber leading to scoring and increased wear.

The same gun with a larger capacity hopper was used as a tank machine gun in 1931 with the name Type 91. The time taken to re-load and the limited ammunition capacity made a poor tank gun.

In 1927 General Nambu formed the Nambu Armament Manufacturing Company at Tokyo. Here he developed in 1932 the Type 92 medium machine gun. This was not a new weapon but an improved version of the Type 3 which itself came from the 1914 Hotchkiss. He chambered the Type 92 gun for a new cartridge, the type 92, which was of 7.7mm calibre semi-rimless.

The expression "semi-rimless" may be unfamiliar to some readers. It means that there was a cannelure around the head of the case for the extractor to grip but the diameter of the base of the round was less than that in front of the cannelure. This base diameter was, nevertheless, larger than a conventional rimless round of which the current NATO 7.62mm round is an example. In 1939 the Japanese introduced a 7.7mm round which was rimless and this round also could be fired by the Type 92 machine gun.

The Type 92 MMG was a very heavy gun weighing 122lbs with its tripod, which was far greater than comparable guns—even water cooled guns—in other armies. The gun was carried by three men in action. One held the forked tube at the rear of the tripod and the others inserted carrying poles in tubes welded to the tripod feet (*205*) and the three men carried the gun from one fire position to another.

The Type 1 was introduced in 1942 weighing only 70lb on its tripod which enabled it to be carried in the same way. It still had the Hotchkiss 30 round feed strip so it can be seen that even in 1942 the Japanese were still using the 1914 Hotchkiss modified through Types 3, 92 and 1.

In 1936 Nambu introduced the Type 96 Light machine gun. This replaced the Type 11 and was a great improvement. The hopper was replaced by a 30 round box magazine, the gun had a quick change barrel and the 6.5mm cartridge was oiled, not on the gun but by an oiler built into the magazine loader. It was often used with a 2½ magnification telescope mounted on the top left hand side of the body.

The next machine gun was the Type 97 introduced for use in armoured fighting vehicles to replace the Type 91. This gun was a copy of the Czech Zb 26 from which the Bren was derived. It fired the new 7.7 rimless round known as Type 99 but was magazine fed which detracted from its performance. Throughout World War II this was the standard

Japanese tank gun. Its shortcomings were recognized and the Japs worked on modifying the Browning aircraft machine gun, which was belt fed, for tank use. The war ended before this gun, designated the Type 4, came into service.

Nambu produced an improved light machine gun called the Type 99 in 1939. It fired the 7.7mm Type 99 rimless round. It was an improved Type 96 built to closer tolerance, with an adjustable cartridge head space and abolished the need to lubricate the cartridge. It is really quite remarkable that the lubricated case should have remained in service right up to this time. This became the standard LMG in the Japanese Armies in the Second World War.

The Japanese weapon and ammunition production system seems to have been quite chaotic. For example the Army, Navy and Air Force never standardised on any one round nor did they worry about weapon nomenclature.

As an example of this the "Type 92" was not only the name for the 7.7mm medium machine gun already mentioned—which fired either the 7.7 semi-rimless or rimless rounds but was also used as the name of the Naval Lewis ground gun and Naval Air Force gun which fired a totally different 7.7mm rimmed round which was interchangeable with the British .303 round. This system—or lack of it—led to immense logistic problems for the Japanese armies.

There were a number of other guns employed by the Japanese. These include the 7.7mm Type 99 which was the .303 Vickers aircraft machine gun, the 12.7mm Type 1 which was the .5in Browning. This Browning was also scaled up as a 20mm aircraft gun.

The French 13.2mm Hotchkiss—a belt fed aircraft gun—was sold to the Japanese in 1933 but the French Government would not release details of the feed system so the Japanese adopted it as a 30 round strip fed gun for anti-aircraft use and called it the Type 93 (1933). It was a standard Hotchkiss design with radial fins all the way along the barrel, firing at 450 rounds a minute and was used not only for anti-aircraft fire in single and twin mounts but also as a ground gun. It was also used on occasion in armoured fighting vehicles.

After World War II, the Japanese defence forces had American equipment for many years. Dr Kawamura of Nittoku Metal Industries designed two machine guns in .30–06 calibre and later a machine gun in 7.62mm NATO (*209–211*). This gun, the model 63, is a conventional gas operated GPMG and has now been adopted in the Japanese forces.

CHAPTER THIRTEEN

Russian Machine Guns

THE FIRST GUN adopted by the Russians was the Gatling. In 1871 General Gorloff headed a mission to Hartford, Connecticut, to the Gatling Machine Gun Co, to supervise the inspection of an order for 400 guns. In accordance with Russian practice his name was stamped on each weapon and as a result the generic term for "machine gun" in Russian was taken to be "Gorloff". The Gatling fired the standard Russian infantry cartridge which was the 4.2 line. The "line" was a linear dimension unique to the Russians and persisted until the Revolution when it was abolished and metric measure adopted. The 4.2 line cartridge was approximately 10.6mm. The Gatling was later manufactured in Russia.

In 1887 Hiram S. Maxim came to St Petersburg to demonstrate his gun. No one there had grasped that the operating energy came from the propellant gases and at first it was believed that the crank handle had to be manipulated by hand. When the gun fired 333 rounds in half a minute the Russians were very impressed but their machinery for procurement was very cumbersome and it was a considerable while before they ordered guns from the Maxim Machine Gun Co. These guns were made in England. Spare barrels were manufactured at the Russian arsenal at Tula and it was not until 1905 that complete guns were made in Russia. The bronze water jacket resulted in an empty gun weight of 69lb. The 1910 model was lightened by the use of a steel jacket and this gun weighing 54lb served the Russian forces throughout two world wars. Lt Col. Chinn quotes Russian production of this gun in the one year, 1944, as 270 000 weapons.

The Russians also purchased a number of the early Madsen model 1903 light machine guns and when the Russo-Japanese war was fought in 1904 the Infantry gun was the Maxim and the cavalry had the Madsen. The Russians however did not learn from their defeat and the Great War in 1914 found them ill-prepared. They placed large orders in the USA where the Colt Company manufactured Vickers guns in 7.62mm for the Russian '08 7.62mm × 54 rimmed round and the Marlin-Rockwell Corporation produced for them the Colt model 1895, the "potato digger".

After the War the new regime decided to develop its own armament industry during the first Five Year Plan. In 1924 a Design office was set up headed by Vladimir Grigorevich Federov. Federov had already designed an automatic rifle, the "Automat" which although very complicated had been produced at the Sestorets factory in 1916 in small numbers totalling 3 000 in all. He started his military career as a Captain in the Foot Guards and was posted to the Officers School at Orenienbaum where weapon testing was carried out. At Orenienbaum he met Vasilry Degtyarev who had been at the Tula factory and took him to help at Sestorets. He selected Degtyarev to be his chief assistant at the Design Office at Kovov.

Over a period of years various designs were produced by Shpitalkny who concentrated on aircraft machine guns, by Beresin, and most important of all by Degtyarev.

Degtyarev Machine Guns
Degtyarev started work on an original design of machine gun in 1921. His gun was known as the DP where D stands for his name and P for "Infantry" and it was adopted in 1926. The DA—aircraft—was brought out in 1928, the DT—tank—in 1929, and the DK (Degtyarev Heavy) in 1934. In 1938 he collaborated with Shpagin to produce a 12.7mm (.5in) Anti-aircraft machine gun.

The DP was produced in 1933 at Tula and was tried out in the Spanish Civil War with considerable success.

All the Degtyarev guns are gas operated and they are basically the same gun with variations according to the role. They were designed to be produced by semi-skilled labour and all have a very rough finish. A description of the Infantry gun, the DP, covers the salient features of all the types. The Russian 7.62 rimmed round is held in a 47 round flat drum magazine placed on top of the gun. Unlike the Lewis magazine it is not gun driven but spring operated. The barrel change which is a feature of all the guns after the first model, is not very quick to operate because the flash hider and gas cylinder nut have to be removed before the cylinder can be taken off to allow the securing pins to be removed before the barrel can be screwed off. The system of locking is common to all models. The bolt is carried on the piston extension and there are two projecting bolt lugs which engage in recesses in the body. As the piston continues to move, after chambering is completed, it drives between these locking pieces which are forced outwards.

The Degtyarev designs served the Soviet armed forces well during World War II. They were reliable, sturdy, easily operated and could be produced in large numbers. After the war they were issued to the satellite countries and then to Korea and Viet Nam where they are still used. The US Forces in Viet Nam are still encountering these weapons and their continued use is a great testimony to Degtyarev's skill.

The first new gun to appear in Europe after the defeat of the Germans was the Degtyarev RP 46, known as the Company machine gun. It is a standard DP with a heavier barrel and modified to take both the 47 round drum or a 50 round continuous metal belt without any modification. It was considered when it first appeared to be of considerable importance but somehow it has not lived up to expectations. Few have been seen in Europe either with the Russian or satellite armies and whilst some have been encountered in South East Asia the numbers have not been large.

The large, rimmed, '08 pattern 7.62mm round with a case length of 54mm was used in the rifle, LMG and MMG. It was ballistically efficient but the length and more particularly the rim, made it poorly adapted for automatic operation. The rim made it difficult for the round to be fed directly into the chamber from a belt and tended to cause mis-feeds in a box magazine. The powerful round led to a heavy weapon and the high impulse made it difficult to control. The Russians had observed the German 7.92mm Kurz round and learned from the MP 44 Assault Rifle and at the cessation of hostilities they produced a new intermediate sized round—the M43—in 7.62 calibre with a case length of 39mm but lighter and with a smaller charge than the old round. A new family of weapons was produced and the Light machine gun was the RPD (Ruchnoi Pelemet Degtyarev). This was a light weight belt fed gun embodying the typical Degtyarev locking system simplified but unchanged in principle. There was no barrel change arrangement and the drill book insisted on the necessity of keeping the practical rate of fire down to 80–100 rounds per minute. This gun lacks power and when firing uphill and lifting a long belt, stoppages are common. It is in process of being superseded by the RPK.

The Degtyarev 12.7mm guns

The DK gun appeared in 1934. It was introduced only in prototype form and was the basis for the next heavy machine gun which appeared in 1938. This was the D. Sh. K. and it was designed jointly by Degtyarev and Shpagin. It used the Russian rimless 12.7mm (.5in) cartridge. The combination of the initials of the two designers arose from the fact that Degtyarev was responsible for the general arrangement and in particular the locking system and firing mechanism while Shpagin designed the feed arrangements. The "K" stands for "heavy". The use of the rimless round means that when it has been stripped from the link in the rotary feed, the bolt can drive it straight into the chamber. This gun was used for AA defence in 1941–1945 by all Russian units and it played a prominent part in Korea where it was used for ground defence.

The rotary Shpagin feed was removed and replaced by a system similar to Degtyarev's 1934 feed which is a bigger version of that used in the 7.62mm RP 46. This gun, the M 1938/46 is used as an AA gun on current Russian tanks and APCs and is now being introduced as the co-axial machine gun on the Russian main battle tank.

The Goryunov M43 Medium Machine Gun

The Soviet designer Peter Maximovitch Goryunov produced the first successor to the Maxim, in 1943.

He used a locking system which in principle is the same as that used in the Bren but instead of lifting up the rear of the breech block into a recess in the body the block is tilted to the right at the back and locked into the body. It is a gas operated gun with the feed system operated directly from the piston in what is probably the simplest arrangement produced for any gun. The barrel is massive but can yet be changed readily. One of the features of the gun is the lack of springs. The return spring and its telescopic rod are the only large springs used. The feed mechanism is very unusual. Since the old '08 rimmed round is used it is almost imperative to withdraw it backwards from the belt but since the bolt locking is achieved by tilting the block, the conventional T slot used by Maxim and Browning cannot be used. Instead Goryunov employed two metal claws which pull the round out and a spring loaded arm to transfer it down to the plane of the chamber. Using this system the gun will function stoppage free upside down or on one side.

The M43 was originally produced with a central cocking handle and a plain barrel and was mounted on a Sokolov type mount. Later versions were used for co-axial mounting in tanks and the cocking handle was then placed on the right of the gun which was given a longitudinally finned barrel.

It is still the current Russian MMG. Its first nomenclature was the M43 and it is now called the SGM. It has probably been the most successful air cooled medium machine gun developed by any country excepting only the .3 Browning.

The Kalashnikov Machine Guns

The introduction of the 7.62mm M43 intermediate round led to the provision of a new Russian automatic rifle—the AK-47. This was modified in the AKM and finally the weapon itself was used as the basis of a new light machine gun—the RPK. The LMG has a heavier barrel than the rifle and has either a 40 round box magazine or a 75 round drum magazine. It is an extremely light but effective arm. The rotating bolt mechanism is exactly the same as the AK rifle and if the cartridge head space lies within prescribed limits, the bolt can be interchanged. Although the lack of a barrel change system must curtail the volume of sustained fire, the chrome plated barrel and the low heat input permit a continuous rate of 80–100rpm.

The PK GPMG. This is the latest Russian rifle round weapon. It employs the old rimmed '08 round with a Goryunov M43 type feed. The same rotating bolt as the AKM, RPK and the Dragunov sniper's rifle is used. This is the first GPMG the Soviet Union has ever had. It comes at an interesting point in weapon development when the Western powers are adopting a small calibre 5.56mm round and departing from the concept of the GPMG towards a light, small calibre machine gun for the Infantry section and a heavier 7.62mm machine gun for vehicle use and sustained fire. When used on a tripod the gun is called the PKS and for tank use, with solenoid firing, it is the PKT. The entire range of Infantry small arm is now of Kalashnikov design.

The KPV Heavy Machine Gun

The 14.5mm KPV was designed by Vladimirov who achieved acclaim with Shpitalny for the Shvak 20mm aircraft cannon (qv). The KPV is a recoil operated gun—the first ground gun so operated since the Maxim—with a rotating bolt of sophisticated design. It fires the PTR round designed for an anti-tank rifle of World War II vintage, with armour piercing incendiary tracer projectiles of high velocity. The gun has been the standard anti-aircraft gun for mobile units for some years, mounted as a twin towed system—the ZU2—and a quadruple arrangement on a self propelled chassis with on mount radar, the ZU4. It is now going into APCs as the anti-APC gun.

The 23mm Zu 23

This gun has been used as an AA gun in a similar way to the KPV 14.5mm. Much speculation was aroused in 1968, when it was observed on a Hungarian armoured car, as to whether the Soviet APCs would be armed at a future date with this high velocity gun in the same way as the British propose to use the RARDEN 30mm gun.

The 23mm Zu 23 is a gas operated gun based on a German Krieghoff design incorporating a rising lock. It is a very accurate light weight weapon and its future employment is a matter of great interest.

Soviet Aircraft Guns

Shkas. In the early 1930s the Russians produced a very efficient but complicated series of guns called the Shkas. It first appeared in 1932 as the model 426 and as the KM-33 in a flexible mount in 1933, followed by improved versions the KM-35, 36 and model 1941 in those years. All these guns were in 7.62mm but using a special aircraft cartridge. The name Shkas comes from the designers, **Sh**pitalny and **K**omaritsky with the 'a' denoting 'aircraft' and the 's' meaning high speed. It was tested in the Spanish Civil War and used throughout World War II and in Korea.

The gun uses features taken from other guns but combines them very efficiently to produce a reliable but complicated weapon, firing 1 800 rounds a minute at 2 750ft/second. The ejection and buffer come from the Maxim, the "bird-cage" feed from the Polish designer Szakats, and the bolt from the Berthier. It is gas operated and the rounds from the belt feed are transferred to the feed cage which holds the rounds and the ejection is in two stages—out of the bolt way and on the next stroke out of the gun.

Shvak. This gun was designed in the late 1930s by Shpitalny and Vladimirov. It is a 20mm gun originally mounted in 1942 on the engine of fighter aircraft and designated the MP. Due to mounting problems it was then positioned in the wing as the KP in 1943 with a flexible version known as the TP. The synchronised version was the SP. A few guns were made in 12.7mm but production was curtailed.

The Shvak is of similar design to the Shkas but with the gas cylinder below the barrel. Firing at 750 rounds a minute with a muzzle velocity of 2 650ft/second it had two barrel lengths, with a blast tube screw threaded to the muzzle. It was a very effective gun.

Beresin. The Russians captured a number of Finnish Lahti 20mm cannon in 1940 and these were re-designed in 12.7mm by Beresin. Again there was a series of guns starting with BS in 1940 which was a fixed gun followed by the UBT as a turret mounted flexible gun in 1941 and the UBK (fixed) and UBS (synchronised) in 1942. It was cheaply made with no provision for factory repair but discarded when unserviceable. It was a successful gun firing at 1 000 rds/minute and a muzzle velocity of 2 800ft/second. It was gas operated and fired the same round as the D. Sh. K with a different belt.

When the 12.7 round became ineffective due to the German armouring of aircraft, the gun was converted in 1942 to 23mm by Volkov and Yartsev and the resulting high velocity gun was known as the VYa.

NS. The Russian designers Nudelman and Suranov produced in 1943 a 37mm short recoil operated aircraft cannon used on the Stormovik. Nudelman designed the gun and Suranov the feed. In 1947 Nudelman produced a 23mm version, identical in all features except the calibre. This gun was based on the German MG-151 with a rotating bolt head and operated by short recoil. It fired at 700 rounds a minute with a muzzle velocity of 2 850ft/second. One of the interesting features was that the gun could be rear seared or front seared enabling it to be fired either from a closed breech or an open breech. The closed breech firing was required for the synchronised gun and the open breech system produced better cooling and was used on wing mounts and flexible mounts.

Future Developments

The machine guns made by the Russians up to the end of World War II were solid, reliable, heavy weapons designed for production by semi-skilled labour and with no unnecessary refinement in their finish.

Since 1945 there has been a change in outlook. Although trusty, well tried designs like the Goryunov M43 have been retained and developed, the trend has been to produce new designs by Kalashnikov which have been at least the equal of anything produced in the West. The RPK with its well finished components and interchangeability of working parts and magazines with the rifle has been a typical example. The new General Purpose Machine Gun is a well designed, carefully made weapon and this, the latest machine gun is said to be lighter, as accurate and as well produced as anything NATO can offer.

The Russian M43 intermediate round of 7.62 mm × 39 has given the Russians a great advantage over the NATO countries, with their heavier round, in producing light weight weapons. They have experimented with their own .223 round (5.56mm) but appear to have no intention of adopting it into service.

Whatever the future may bring we can be certain that the days of rough and ready machine guns are gone for ever.

Credits For Illustrations

Aircraft Armaments Inc: Fig. 72.

Associated Press: Fig. 218, 221.

Birmingham Museum: Fig. 17.

BSA Guns Ltd: Fig. 46, 117, 118, 119, 121, 122, 129, 139, 140, 193.

Cadillac Gage Co: Fig. 70.

Colts Patent Firearms Corp: Fig. 68, 69.

Commandant RMCS: Fig. 4, 6, 10, 39, 40, 53, 58, 59, 102, 113, 114, 128, 162, 165, 166, 167, 171, 172, 180, 186, 187, 190, 197, 198, 215, 217, 222, 228, 231, 232, 233, 234, 236.

Crown Copyright: Fig. 54, 62, 145, 146, 147, 148, 149, 150, 152, 153, 154, 155, 214, 226.

D. Edwards: Fig. 30 .

N. Flayderman & Co. New Milford, Connecticut: Fig. 7.

FN Ltd: Fig. 34, 35, 36, 37, 142, 143, 144.

Heckler and Koch Ltd: Fig. 194.

Imperial War Museum: Fig. 41, 42, 47, 78, 93, 99, 107, 112, 158, 159, 182, 185, 196, 216, 227.

Infantry: Fig. 56.

International General Electric Company of New York: Fig. 60, 61, 65, 66.

Dr. Masaya Kawamura: Fig. 203, 205, 209, 210, 211.

Madsen Arms Co: Fig. 212.

National Army Museum: Fig. 33.

NWM de Kruithoorn: Fig. 64, 71.

Oerlikon-Buhrle Ltd: Fig. 240.

J Parker: Fig. 2, 3, 9.

Pattern Room Committee, RSAF Enfield: Fig. 5, 13, 22, 24, 28, 48, 49, 67, 79, 80, 81, 82, 83, 84, 85, 86, 87, 88, 89, 90, 91, 92, 94, 95, 96, 98, 100, 101, 103–106, 108–111, 120, 123, 125, 130, 131, 132, 133, 135, 136, 137, 138, 141, 157, 163, 164, 173, 174, 175, 176, 182, 195, 199, 200, 201, 202, 204, 206, 207, 208, 219, 220.

Radio Times Hulton Picture Library: Fig. 160, 170.

Rheinmetall: Fig. 181, 191, 192.

Rolls-Royce Ltd: Fig. 134.

Rotunda Museum, Woolwich: Fig. 11, 18, 20, 21.

S.I.G.: Fig. 237, 238, 239.

The Book of the Machine Gun by permission of Hugh Rees Ltd.: Fig. 16, 31, 75, 156.

The Gatling Gun by permission of Arco Publishing Co: Fig. 12, 14, 15, 19.

Tower of London: Fig. 8, 23.

United Press International: Fig. 44, 115.

US Army Photograph: Fig. 43, 55.

US Marine Corps Museum: Fig. 25.

Vickers Limited: Fig. 27, 29, 76, 77, 97, 124.

John Wiley & Sons, New York: Fig. 1.

Tabulated Machine Gun Data

Name of Weapon	Ammunition	Method of Operation	Method of Locking	Feed and Capacity	Cooling	Weight (lbs)	Rate of Fire (Rpm)	Muzzle Velocity ft/s	Remarks
American Guns Armalite AR-10 LMG	7.62mm NATO	Gas-direct action (No piston)	Rotating Bolt	Belt 50	Air	9¼	700	2 800	AR-10 rifle with belt feed and strengthened body. Heavier barrel.
Colt MG M1895	6mm Lee .30-40 Krag .30-06 .30-06	Gas-swinging arm	Tilting Block	Belt 250	Air	40	400	2 550 2 000 2 400	Potato-digger
Browning MG Model 1910	"	Recoil	Projecting Lug	Belt 250	Water	41	450-600	2 800	Prototype of Browning MG Model 1917
Colt Automatic machine rifle R75	"	Gas-piston	Link-upwards	Mag 20	Air	20¼	400	2 400	Commercial equivalent to M1918 A1
Browning Automatic Rifle M1918	"	"	"	"	"	16	400	2 400	
Browning Automatic Rifle M1918 A1	"	"	"	"	"	18½	"	"	BAR Bipod on gas cylinder
Browning Automatic Rifle M1918 A2	"	"	"	"	"	21	300	"	Bipod attached to flash eliminator stock rest in butt
Browning Automatic Rifle M1922	"	"	"	"	"	22	400	"	Finned barrel with bipod attached. Stock rest clamped to butt
Colt "Monitor" Auto Machine Rifle R80	"	"	"	"	"	16¼	"	"	Improved R75. Used mainly by US Police
Colt Auto Gun M1914 (F and F model)	"	Gas-Swinging Arm	Tilting Block	Belt 250	Water	40	600	2 800	Commercial model of MG M1914. Modified M1895.
Colt MG M1914	"	"	"	"	Air	40	600	2 800	Modified M1895
Colt MG M1917	"	"	"	"	Water	35	"	"	Modified M1914
Marlin aircraft MG M1917	"	Gas Piston	"	"	Air	22	850-1 000	2 750	Modified M1895
Marlin Tank MG M1917	"	"	"	"	"	"	600	2 750	Modified aircraft MG 1917 with aluminium radiator of Lewis type
Colt MG MG38 and 38B	"	Recoil	Projecting Lug	Belt 250	Water	41	450-600	2 800	Commercial models of Browning MG 1917 and 1917 A1
Browning MG M 1917	"	"	"	"	"	"	"	"	
Browning MG M1917A1	"	"	"	"	"	"	"	"	Modified M1917. Standard ground gun in WWII. (Weight included water).
Browning aircraft MG M1918	"	Recoil with gas assistance	"	"	Air	30½	1 100	2 750	

Name of Weapon	Ammunition	Method of Operation	Method of Locking	Feed and Capacity	Cooling	Weight (lbs)	Rate of Fire (Rpm)	Muzzle Velocity ft/s	Remarks
American Guns (Cont.)									
Browning aircraft MG M1918 M1 (Fixed and Flexible models)	.30-06	Recoil with gas assistance	Projecting Lug	Belt 250	Air	30½	1 100	2 750	Modified M1918
Browning aircraft MG M1919 (Fixed and Flexible models)	,,	,,	,,	,,	,,	30	1 100	2 750	Improved M1918 M1
Colt Light Aircraft MG40 (Fixed and Flexible models)	,,	,,	,,	,,	,,	22 (Fixed) 24 (Flexible)	1 200	2 750	Adopted in .303 for British fighter aircraft in 1935. Prototype of Colt MG 40-2
Colt Light Aircraft MG40-2 (Fixed and Flexible models)	,,	,,	,,	,,	,,		1 200	2 750	Commercial model of Browning aircraft MG M2
Browning Aircraft MG M2	,,	,,	,,	,,	,,	21.5 Fixed 23 Flexible	1 350	2 800	Improved Browning Aircraft MG M1919
Browning Tank MG M1919	,,	,,	,,	,,	,,	33	550	2 800	M1919 with brackets for telescopic sight
Browning Tank MG M1919 A1	,,	,,	,,	,,	,,	,,	,,	,,	Used in AFVs and by US Cavalry
Browning Tank MG M1919 A2 (Flexible)	,,	,,	,,	,,	,,	31	,,	,,	
Browning Tank MG M1919 A3 (Flexible)	,,	,,	,,	,,	,,	31	,,	,,	M1919 with hole in cover latch for sight. Few made.
Browning Tank MG M1919 A4 (Flexible)	,,	,,	,,	,,	,,	,,	,,	,,	Improved M1919 A2 with barrel length increased from 18.6in to 24in
Browning Tank MG M1919 A5 (Fixed)	,,	,,	,,	,,	,,	,,	,,	,,	M1919 A4 fixed modified for Westinghouse Gyro stabilised tank mounting.
Browning Tank MG3C M2 Heavy Barrel (Fixed and Flexible)	,,	,,	,,	,,	,,	,,	,,	,,	M2 Aircraft (Fixed) fitted with heavy barrel for right hand feed in AFVs. Experimental model.
Browning MG M1919 A6	,,	,,	,,	,,	,,	32.5	500	,,	Ground gun in WW II. Modified 1919 A4 with bipod, shoulder stock and carrying handle.
Browning MG M1919 A4E1	,,	,,	,,	,,	,,	31	500	,,	Post WW II development of the M1919 A4 with retracting slide similar to M1919 A5.
Browning MG M1918	.5	Recoil	Projecting Lug	Belt	Water	62 w/o water 78 w/water	450	2 300	Barrel length 30.5in. 16 pints of water.
Browning aircraft	.5	,,	,,	,,	Air	60	500	,,	Feed from left only.

Name of Weapon	Ammunition	Method of Operation	Method of Locking	Feed and Capacity	Cooling	Weight (lbs)	Rate of Fire (Rpm)	Muzzle Velocity ft/s	Remarks
American Guns (Cont.) MG M1921 (Fixed and Flexible)									
Browning MG M1921	·5	Recoil	Projecting Lug	Belt	Water	79	500	2 840	Anti-aircraft. Feed from left only. Barrel length 36in.
Browning MG M1921 A1	,,	,,	,,	,,	,,	76	,,	,,	Modified M1921.
Browning MG M2 aircraft basic	,,	,,	,,	,,	Air	61	850	,,	This gun can be modified by the addition of extra assemblies. Barrel weight 9.8lb. Basic length 36in.
Browning MG M2 aircraft. Heavy barrel Fixed	,,	,,	,,	Belt 110	Air	84	550	2 930	Barrel weight 27lb. Barrel length 45in.
Browning MG M2 aircraft Heavy barrel Turret type	,,	,,	,,	,,	,,	81	575	2 930	Barrel weight 27lb. Barrel length 45in.
Browning MG M2 Ground-flexible	,,	,,	,,	,,	,,	84	575	2 930	Barrel weight 23lb. Barrel length 45in.
Browning MG M2 Anti-aircraft	·5	Recoil	Projecting Lug	Belt 110	Water	100 w/o water 121 w/ water	650	2 930	Barrel weight 15.2lb Barrel length 45in. 20 pints of water
Browning MG M3 Aircraft	,,	,,	,,	Belt	Air	69	1 250	2 840	Barrel length 36ins
De Knight MG	.30-06	Gas Piston	Pivoting Lock	Belt	Water	38½	600	2 228	Based on Birkigt Type 404
Hispano-Suiza USA M1	20mm	Gas to unlock Blow back to operate	Projecting Lug	Belt	Air	105	600	2 750	
Hispano-Suiza USA M2	,,	,,	,,	,,	,,	112	600	2 750	Strengthened body
Hispano-Suiza USA M3	,,	,,	,,	,,	,,	87	650	2 670	Based on T25–29 series. Barrel shortened 15in.
Hotchkiss (Benét-Mercié)	8mm Lebel	Gas Piston	Fermature nut	Strip	,,	27	650	2 296	
Johnson M1941	.30-06	Recoil to unlock Blowback to operate	Rotating bolt head	Magazine 20	Air	13	400	2 800	
Johnson M1944 (T48)	.30-06	Recoil to unlock Blowback to operate	Rotating Bolt Head	Magazine 20	Air	14.7	450-700	2 800	Fires SS from closed breech. Fires auto from open breech.
Marlin (Modified M1895)	,,	Gas-piston	Link upwards	Belt 250	Air	22	850-1 000	2 750	Fires SS from closed breech. Fires auto from open breech.
Maxim M1904	,,	Recoil	Toggle	Drum 47 and 96	Water	40	600	2 750	
Lewis	,,	Gas-piston	Rotating Bolt	,,	Air	25	450-500	2 750	
M39 (aircraft)	20mm			Belt	Air		1 900	3 450	

Name of Weapon	Ammunition	Method of Operation	Method of Locking	Feed and Capacity	Cooling	Weight (lbs)	Rate of Fire (Rpm)	Muzzle Velocity ft/s	Remarks
American Guns (Cont.)									
M60 GPMG	7.62mm	Gas-piston	Rotating Bolt	Air	Belt 200	23	600	2 800	
M61 Vulcan (6 Barrels) Aircraft	20mm	Electrical	Projecting Lug	Belt	Air	255	Up to 6 000	3 450	
M73 Tank Machine gun	7.62mm	Recoil with gas assistance	Sliding Block	Belt 250	Air	29·3	500	2 800	
M85 Tank Machine Gun	·5	Recoil	2 Projecting lugs	Belt	Air	61.5	400 and 1,050	2 840	
Minigun (6 barrels) (Aircraft)	7.62mm	Electrical	Rotating Bolt Head	"	"	45.5 (gun only)	Up to 6 000	2 800	
Minigun (prototypes only) 6 barrels	5·56mm (.223)	Electrical	"	"	"	26	Up to 10 000	3 300	
XM 197 Aircraft 3 Barrels	20mm	Electrical	Projecting Lug	"	"	146	Up to 1 500	3 400	
Oerlikon	20mm	Blowback	None-Inertia block and Advanced Primer Ignition	Magazine 60	"	141	475	2 725	
Sedgley LMG	.30-06	Gas Piston	Rotating Bolt	Belt	"	23.5	600	2 800	
Stoner LMG	5·56mm (.223)	Gas piston	Rotating Bolt Head	Belt	"	11.7	700	3 250	
XM 207 Stoner MMG	5·56mm (.223)	Gas piston	Rotating Bolt Head	100 Belt	Air	10.2	650-850	3 250	
Vickers M1918 Aircraft	.30-06	Recoil-gas assisted	Toggle joint	Belt 250	"	25	800-900	2 800	
Vickers Mk I Ground	.30-06	Recoil-gas assisted	"	"	Water	40	450-5 500	2 750	
Vickers Aircraft Anti-Balloon Gun (Colt manufacture)	11mm	Recoil-gas assisted	Toggle joint	Belt	Air	45	600	2 400	Converted from Russian orders in 1917, by Colt
British Guns									
Beardmore-Farquhar	.303	Gas-piston and spring	Rotating Bolt Head	Drum 77	Air	16¼	450-550	2 427	
BESA Mk I	7·92mm	Gas-piston	Tilting block	Belt 225	Air	47	450 and 750	2 700	Barrel recoils on firing to reduce trunnion load on mounting
BESA Mk 2	"	"	"	"	"	48	"	"	Difference in Mks due to rate controller and simplified manufacture
BESA Mk 3	"	"	"	"	"	54	450 only	"	
BESA Mk 3*	"	"	"	"	"	53.5	"	"	
BESA 15mm Mk. I	15mm	Gas piston	Vertical Projecting lugs	Belt .25	Air	125·5	400	2 685	
BESAL (Faulkoner) Mk I LMG	.303		"	Magazine 30	"	20	600	2 440	Cocked like a Bren gun
Mk 2 LMG	.303	Recoil	Rotating bolt sleeve	Drum Magazine 37	Air or Water	22	400	"	Cocked like a BESA. Heavy barrel
BSA Model 1924 Aircraft	·5		"	Flat Drum 99		46	400	2 600	Barrel recoils 2¼in
BSA Adams Willmot	·303	Gas piston	Tilting block	Belt 200	"	20	900	2 440	Converted Bren
BSA GPMG	7.62mm		"		"	25	750	2 750	

Name of Weapon	Ammunition	Method of Operation	Method of Locking	Feed and Capacity	Cooling	Weight (lbs)	Rate of Fire (Rpm)	Muzzle Velocity ft/s	Remarks
British Guns (Cont.)									
Bren LMG Mk I	.303	Gas-piston	Tilting block	Magazine 30 or Drum 200	Air	22¼	500	2 440	Barrel 25in 6¼lb
Mk 2	,,	,,	,,	Magazine 30	,,	23¼	550	2 440	Barrel 25in 6¼lb
Mk 3	,,	,,	,,	,,	,,	19.3	500	2 440	Barrel 22¼in 5lb
Mk 4	,,	,,	,,	,,	,,	19.1	520	2 440	Barrel 22¼in 5lb
L4 A1-4	7.62mm	Recoil-gas assisted	Projecting lug	Belt 250	Air	20	600	2 750	7.62mm conversion of Mk 3 Bren
Browning .3in	30-06	Recoil	,,	,,	Air	32.5	400-500	2 800	Used in British AFVs
Browning Aircraft	.303	Gas to unlock	Projecting lug	Magazine 60	,,	26.5	1 200	2 440	Mk 1, 2 and 2*
Hispano-Suiza Mk 1-2 Aircraft	20mm	Blowback to operate			,,	109	650	2 880	
Hotchkiss Mk I	.303	Gas-piston	Fermature nut	Strip 30	,,	27	650	2 440	Mk 1* takes strip or belt. Mk 2 is tank version of Mk 1*
L7A1-2 GPMG	7.62mm	Gas-piston	Link-downwards	Belt 200	Air	23½	750-1 000	2 750	Derived from FN MAG. A2 has double sear
L8 Tk MG (Fixed)	7.62mm NATO	,,	,,	,,	,,	24	,,	2 750	Differs from GPMG in gas regulator, no sights, no butt, no barrel change handle, heavy barrel. Solenoid.
L37 Tk MG	7.62mm	,,	,,	,,	,,	24	,,		As L8A1 but has butt and sights
L20 Helicopter Machine gun Flexible	7.62mm	,,	,,	Belt	,,	24	,,	2 750	Heavy barrel, L7 gas regulator. Solenoid fired. No butt
Lewis .303 Mk I Ground	.303	,,	Rotating bolt	Drum 47	Air	27	500-600	2 400	
Air Mk II	,,	,,	,,	Drum 96	,,	23	500-600	2 440	
Air Mk III	,,	,,	,,	,,	,,	23	500-600	2 440	
Lewis Model 1918 Air	.30-06	,,	,,	,,	,,	22	800	2 800	Savage
Lewis .303 Mk IV Ground	.303	Gas piston	Rotating bolt	Drum 47	,,	23	500-600	2 440	Homeguard
Lewis .303 Mk IV Ground (Modified)	.45	Recoil	Rotating crank	Magazine 30	Air	23	600	2 440	
Maxim, First Model 1884				Vertical then Flat Drum then Belt 333	Water	60	1-600	1 200	Once at the Imperial War Museum, now at the US Marine Corps. Museum Quantico, Virginia
Maxim	.303	Blowback	Toggle joint	Belt	Water	40	600	2 440	
Oerlikon Mk 1	20mm		None-inertia block and advanced primer ignition	Magazine 60	Air	141	475	2 725	Swiss made
Mk 2	,,	,,	As Oerlikon	,,	,,	,,	,,	,,	UK or US made
Mk 4	,,	,,	,,	,,	,,	,,	,,	,,	US made
Polsten	30mm	,,	Sliding block	Magazine 30 2 Clips of 3	,,	121	450	2 440	Limited auto fire at 8orpm for AA
RARDEN XL21E2		Long recoil			,,	220	Single shot	3 650	
Rolls-Royce Experimental I	.5 US	Recoil	Projecting lugs	Belt	Air	49	960-1 080	2 800	Locking system—improved Degtyarev

Name of Weapon	Ammunition	Method of Operation	Method of Locking	Feed and Capacity	Cooling	Weight (lbs)	Rate of Fire (Rpm)	Muzzle Velocity ft/s	Remarks
British Guns (Cont.)									
Experimental II	.55 Boys ATK	Recoil	Projecting Lugs	Belt	Air	40	960-1080	2800	Prototype only. Designed to produce 7 000rds/hr
Russel Robinson	.5	,,	Sliding block	,,	Air	43	450	,,	Mks I-III L Class
TADEN GPMG	.28	Gas-piston	Tilting block	Belt 100	Air	22	600	2 500	K Class
Vickers Berthier	.303	Gas-piston	,,	Magazine 30	Air	22	600	2 440	
Vickers Gas Operated	.303	,,	,,	Drum Mag 100	,,	21	1 000	2 440	C Class
Vickers MMG Mk I	.303	Recoil-gas assisted	Toggle joint	Belt 250	Water	40	450-550	2 440	Mk I barrel casing with louvres.
Mk I*	.303	,,	,,	,,	Air	38	,,	2 440	Aircraft gun
Mk II	.303	,,	,,	,,	,,	22	,,	2 440	Standard fixed air gun
Mk III	.303	,,	,,	,,	,,	22		2 440	Long flash hider
Mk IV	.303	,,	,,	,,	Water	38	450-500	2 440	Experimental modified Mk I gun for AFV use
Vickers Mk IVb	.303	Recoil-gas assisted	Toggle joint	Belt 250	Water	38	450-500	2 440	Production gun for AFVs
Mk V	.303	,,	,,	,,	Air	22	750	2 440	L or R hand feeds. Fixed aircraft gun
Mk VI	.303	,,	,,	,,	Water	41¾	500	2 440	AFV gun. Not fitted for header tank
Mk VII	.303	,,	,,	,,	,,	47¼		2 440	AFV gun with fitting for header tank
Vickers Class "A"	.303	,,	,,	,,	Air	32¼	450-550	2 440	Left or right feed / Protected heavy aluminium jacketed barrel
Vickers MMG Mk I	.5	Recoil only	,,	Belt 100	Water	55	400	2 600	Experimental ground gun. No muzzle cup
Mk II	.5	,,	,,	,,	,,	58	700	,,	First AFV gun. Selective fire
Mk III	.5	,,	,,	,,	,,	58		,,	Naval service. Ejector tube. Automatic only. Disintegrating link belt.
Mk IV	.5	,,	,,	,,	,,	58	650-700	,,	AFV gun. Ejector tube separate from pistol grip
Mk V	.5	,,	,,	,,	,,	58	700		AFV gun. Valve allows steam to blow off at 10psi
Vickers Class "B"	.5	,,	,,	,,	Air	52	700	3 000	Armoured barrel. For air use.
"D"	.5	,,	,,	,,	Water	55	,,		AA use
French Guns									
AA-52 GPMG	7.5mm	Delayed blowback	2 part-block, lever delay	Belt 200	Air	24	600	2 700	A few chambered for 7.62mm NATO
Berthier M1908	8mm Lebel	Gas-piston	Tilting block	Magazine 30	Air	19	250-400	2 300	Chambered for .30-06 for US use and known as M1918 CSRG
Chauchat LMG Model 1915	8mm Lebel	Long recoil	Rotating Bolt head	Magazine 20	Air	18	240	2 300	Chambered for M24 round
Chatellerault LMG Model 1924-29	7.5mm Rimless	Gas-piston	Tilting block	Magazine 30	Air	22	450-500	2 700	Later modified for M29 round
Chatellerault Tk. MG Model 31	7.5mm Rimless	Gas-piston	Tilting block	Drum Mag. 150	Air	36	500	2 700	Drum on side of gun
Chatellerault Aircraft Gun Model 34-39	7.5mm Rimless	Gas-piston	Tilting block	Belt 250	Air	24	1 300	2 700	

Name of Weapon	Ammunition	Method of Operation	Method of Locking	Feed and Capacity	Cooling	Weight (lbs)	Rate of Fire (Rpm)	Muzzle Velocity ft/s	Remarks
French Guns (Cont.)									
Darne Model 29 Aircraft	7.5mm Rimless	Gas-piston	Tilting block	Belt 250	Air	18½	1 200	2 700	
Hispano-Suiza Type 404 aircraft	20mm	Gas-piston to unlock, blowback to operate	Projecting lug	Drum 60 Belt 200	Air	110	500	2 750	
Hotchkiss Model 1897	8.mm Lebel	Gas-piston	Swinging lock	Strip 30	Air	55	600	2 400	Fermature nut—locking ring. Cartridges beneath strip
Hotchkiss Portative or Benét-Mercié LMG 1909	8.mm Lebel	Gas-piston	Fermature nut	Strip 25	Air	27	650–700	2 400	Chambered for .30-06 for US use
Hotchkiss Model 1914	8.mm Lebel	Gas-piston	Link locking	Strip 30	Air	55	450	2 400	
Hotchkiss Anti-Balloon Gun	12mm	Gas-piston	Link locking	Strip 20	Air	66	450	2 020	
Hotchkiss-Aircraft MG M30	13.2mm	Gas-piston	Link locking	Belt 100	Air		600		
Hotchkiss MG30	25mm	Gas-piston	Projecting lug	Magazine 10	Air	164	175	2 700	Prototype only
Hotchkiss MAS 1950 GPMG	.30-06	Gas-piston	Tilting block	Magazine 30 or Belt 200	Air	22	750	2 750	
Puteaux Model 1905	8mm Lebel	Gas-piston	Swinging Lock	Strip 23	Air	54	650	2 300	Improved 1897 mode Hotchkiss
St Etienne Model 1907	8mm Lebel	Gas-piston driven forward	Swinging Lock	Strip 25	Air	46	500	2 300	
German Guns									
Becker Aircraft Cannon	20mm	Blowback	Inertia block	Magazine 12	Air	66	350	1 570	
Bergman Model 1910 MMG	7.92mm	Recoil	Sliding block	Belt 200	Water	36	550	2 952	
Bergman Model 1915 MMG	7.92mm	,,	,,	,,	Air	34	750–800	2 952	
Dreyse Model 1912 MMG	7.92mm	,,	Hinged block	,,	Water	37½	550–600	2 952	Models 15 and 18 were improvements
Erhardt Aircraft Cannon	20mm	,,	,,	Magazine 20	Air	160	250–300	2 200	Scaled up MG-13
FG-42 LMG	7.92mm	Gas-piston	Rotating bolt	Magazine 20	Air	14	400–450	2 750	Fires SS from closed breech. Fires auto from open breech
Flak 30 AA Cannon	20mm	Recoil	Hinged block	Magazine 20 or 40	Air	141	250	2 950	Made by Rheinmetall
Flak 38 AA Cannon	20mm	Recoil	Rotating bolt Head	Magazine 20	Air	123	450	2 950	Made by Mauser
Gast. Model 1918 Aircraft MG (Twin barrels)	7.92mm	Recoil	Rotating bolt	Drum Mags. 180 each	Air	60	1 800	2 900	Twin barrels each utilising recoil energy from the other

Name of Weapon	Ammunition	Method of Operation	Method of Locking	Feed and Capacity	Cooling	Weight (lbs)	Rate of Fire (Rpm)	Muzzle Velocity ft/s	Remarks
German Guns (Cont.)									
Heckler and Koch HK13	5.56mm (.223)	Delayed Blowback	2 part block-roller delay	Magazine 30	Air	8.0	650	3 200	
HK23 ,,	5.56mm (.223)	,,	,,	Belt	Air	8.0	650	3 200	Experimental
HK12 ,,	7.62M43 Russian	,,	,,	Magazine 30	Air	7½	650	2 200	
Knorr-Bremse Model 35/36	7.92mm	Gas-piston	Tilting block	Magazine 25	Air	19	450–500	2 952	Never used by German Army but supplied to Finland in 1940
Lubbe Air Craft Cannon	20mm	Gas-piston and blowback	Sliding block	Drum Magazine 30	Air	107	360	2 650	Never in service
Maxim Model MMG '08	7.92mm	Recoil	Toggle	Belt 200	Water	40½	600	2 750	
Maxim Model '08–15	7.92mm	,,	,,	Belt 50	Water	31	600	2 750	Lightened '08 with no water circulation
Maxim Tu F (1918)	12.7mm	Recoil	Toggle	Belt 100	Air or water	84	400	2 750	Tu F = Tank und Flieger = tank and aircraft. Never in service
MG3 (1961) GPMG	7.62mm	Recoil-gas assisted	Projecting rollers	Belt 200	Air	24	600 or 1 200	2 750	Modernised MG 42 with bolt giving 2 rates of fire. Called MG 42/59 then MG1, finally MG 3
MG13 (1930) LMG	7.92mm	Recoil, gas assisted	Swinging wedge	Double drum 75	Air	26.4	750	2 750	Modified Dreyse, Model 18
MG15 (1932) Aircraft Rheinmetall	7.92mm	,,	Locking ring	Double drum 75 or belt 250	Air	28	1 000	2 552	Derived from Solothurn MG30. Fixed gun-belt. Flexible mounted gun-drums. Later used as ground LMG
MG17 (1934) Aircraft Rheinmetall	7.92mm	,,	,,	Belt 250	Air	28	1 000	2 552	Improved MG-15
MG34 GPMG Mauser (1934)	7.92mm	Recoil-gas assisted	Rotating bolt head	Belt 250 or double drum 75	Air	24½	750	2 750	Used throughout World War II as Infantry and tank machine gun
MG42 GPMG Mauser (1942)	7.92mm	Recoil-gas assisted	Projecting Rollers	Belt 250	Air	24	1 200	2 750	
MG45 GPMG Mauser (1945)	7.92mm	Delayed blowback	2 part block roller delay	Belt 250	Air	23	650	2 750	Never in service
MG81 Aircraft Mauser (1936)	7.92mm	Short recoil	Rotating bolt head	Belt 250	Air	14	1 250	2 750	Twin barrelled gun based on MG34
MG131 Aircraft Rheinmetall (1938)	13mm	Recoil-gas assisted	Locking ring	Belt 100	Air	40	960	2 560	Electrically fired
MG151 Aircraft Mauser (1936)	20mm	Recoil	Rotating bolt head	Belt 50	Air	93½	725	2 590	Electrically fired
MK-ST-11 Aircraft Rheinmetall (1935)	20mm	,,	Projecting lug	Magazine 20	Air	118	350–380	2 250	AA version known as MK-ST-5
Mk S-18-100 Anti Tank Rheinmetall (1936)	20mm	,,	Locking ring	Magazine 20	Air	80	Single shot only	2 250	Mk-S18-1 000 was improved version

129

Name of Weapon	Ammunition	Method of Operation	Method of Locking	Feed and Capacity	Cooling	Weight (lbs)	Rate of Fire (Rpm)	Muzzle Velocity ft/s	Remarks
Italian Guns									
Breda Model 1924 LMG	6.5mm	Recoil to unlock. Blowback to operate	Locking nut	Magazine 20	Air	20	475	2 080	Oiled cartridge
Breda Model 1928 Aircraft	12.7mm	Recoil		Belt 50	Air	58	400	2 600	Prototype only
Breda Model 1930 LMG	6.5mm	Recoil to unlock. Blowback to operate	Locking nut	Magazine 20	Air	20	500	2 080	Oiled cartridge
Breda Model 1931 Tk HMG and AA	13.2mm	Gas-piston	Vertical sliding block	Magazine 20	Air	27			
Breda Model 1935 MMG	7.7mm	Recoil to unlock. Blowback to operate	Rolling Lock	Belt 250	Air	27	625	2 400	Oiled cartridge. Fired British .303
Breda-Safat Model 1935 Aircraft	7.7mm	Recoil	Pivoting hook	Belt	Air	27	800	2 400	Fired British .303
Breda Model 1937 MMG	8mm	Gas piston	Vertical sliding lock	Strip 20	Air	42½	500	2 600	Oiled cartridge. Empty case replaced in strip
Breda Model 1938	8mm	" "	" "	Magazine 20	Air	42	500	2 600	Oiled cartridge. Ejected spent case
Brixia Model 1920	6.5mm	Short Recoil	Pivoted locking piece	Magazine 50	Water	34	600	2 080	
Fiat Revelli 1914 MMG	6.5mm	Delayed blowback	Swinging wedge	Magazine 50	Water	38	500	2 080	Magazine has 10 compartments each holding 5 rounds. Oiled rounds
Fiat Revelli 1914 Aircraft	6.5mm	" "	" "	" "	Air	30	500	2 080	Aircraft version of Infantry gun
Fiat Revelli 1926 MMG	6.5mm	" "	" "	Magazine 20	Air	30	500	2 080	Oiled rounds. Only 2 000 made
Fiat Revelli 1928 MMG	6.5mm	Recoil	Pivoting hook	Magazine 20	Air	21	500	2 080	Ammunition unlubricated
Fiat Model 1928 Anti-Aircraft	12.7mm	Recoil	" "	" "	Air	60	400	2 080	Prototypes only
Fiat Model 28 Aircraft	7.7mm	Recoil with gas assistance	Pivoting hook	Belt 200	Air	24	800	2 400	A rebuilt 1914 model with fluted chamber
Fiat Model 1935	8mm	Delayed blowback	Swinging wedge	Magazine 50	Air	24	120	2 600	Never in service
Perino Model 1908	7.7mm	Recoil	Tilting block	Strip 25	Water	50	600	2 400	
Scotti Model 1928	7.7mm	Gas to unlock. Blowback to operate	Rotating bolt head	Magazine 20	Air	22	500	2 400	
Scotti Sistar Model 1932	20mm / 6.5mm	Recoil to unlock. Blowback to operate	Toggle joint	Magazine 60 / Belt 250	Air / Air	156 / 22	400 / 700	2 650 / 2 100	Lubricated rounds
Villa Perosa	7.92mm / 9mm	Delayed Blowback	Rotating bolt head	Belt 250 / 2 Magazines of 30	Air / Air	44 / 18	500 / 800	2 700 / 1 200	Two barrels

Name of Weapon	Ammunition	Method of Operation	Method of Locking	Feed and Capacity	Cooling	Weight (lbs)	Rate of Fire (Rpm)	Muzzle Velocity ft/s	Remarks
Japanese Guns									
Hotchkiss M1897	6.5mm	Gas-piston	Swinging lock	Strip 25	Air	55	600	2 434	
Type 3 (1914)	6.5mm	,,	Link-downwards	Strip 30	Air	60	500	2 434	
Type 11 (1922)	6.5mm	,,	Projecting lugs	Hopper 30	Air	22.5	500	2 300	Type 89 is aircraft version
Type 89 (1929)	7.7mm	Recoil-gas assisted	Toggle joint	Belt	Air	27	450	2 400	Aircraft Vickers. Used also in ground service.
Type 91 (1931)	6.5mm	Gas-piston	Projecting lugs	Hopper 30	Air	22.2	500	2 300	Tank gun version of Type 11. Fires Type 92 or 99 ammunition. "Juki"
Type 92 (1932)	7.7mm	,,	Link-downwards	Strip 30	Air	61	500	2 400	
Type 92 (1932)	7.7mm	,,	Rotating bolt	Drum 47	Air	26	600	2 400	Lewis gun. Air and ground
Type 93 (1933)	13.2mm	,,	Link-downwards	Strip 30	Air	145	450	2 210	Hotchkiss M 1932
Type 96 (1936)	6.5mm	Recoil	Rising lock	Box 30	Air	20	550	2 400	Browning mechanism of .5 made in 20mm
Type 96 (1936)	20mm		Projecting lug	Belt	Air	135	450	2 700	Also tank machine gun with armoured cover over barrel.
Type 97 (1937)	7.7mm	Gas-piston	Tilting block	Box 30	Air	26	500	2 400	Bren type mechanism
Type 98 (1938)	7.92mm	Recoil-gas assisted	Locking ring	Saddle drum 75	Air	15½	900	2 750	German MG-15. Aircraft adapted for ground use
Type 99 (1939)	7.7mm	Gas-piston	Rising lock	Box-30	Air	23	850	2 350	Type 99 ammunition only
Type 1 (1941)	7.92mm	,,	Tilting block	Saddle drum 75	Air	36	600	2 750	This first appeared in 1941 as an aircraft gun. Improved next year. Has 2 barrels
Type 1 (1941)	7.7mm	,, ,,	Link-downwards	Strip 30	Air	33½	550	2 400	Type 99 ammunition only
Type 1 (1941)	12.7mm	Recoil	Projecting lug	Belt	Air	61	850	2 800	Browning .5 basic gun
NTK Machine Gun Model 62	7.62mm	Gas-piston	Tilting block	Belt 200	Air	22	550	2 750	Made by Nittoku Metal Industries
Russian Guns									
Beresin BS (1940)	12.7mm	Gas-piston	Projecting lug	Belt	Air	47	1 000	2 800	BS = Beresin Samolenti Beresin aircraft. (Fixed gun) also used as AA
UBT (1941)	12.7mm	,,	,,	,,	,,	49	,,	,,	Aircraft turret gun
UBK (1941)	12.7mm	,,	,,	,,	,,	49	,,	,,	Fixed gun in wing
UBS (1941)	12.7mm	,,	,,	,,	,,	49	,,	,,	Fixed and synchronised
VYA (1942)	23mm	,,	,,	,,	,,	145	650-750	2 974	Scaled up BS by Volkow and Yartsev
Colt Model 1895 1915	7.62mm X 54 R	Gas-swinging arm	Tilting block	Belt 250	,,	40	550	2 650	Manufactured in 1915 by Marlin-Rockwell. Fired the '08 rimmed rd.
Degtyarev DP	7.62mm X 54 R	Gas-piston	Projecting lugs	Flat drum 47	Air	20	500-600	2 770	Infantry gun, prototype in 1924, tested in 1926, produced from 1930 to 1947
DA	7.62mm X 54 R	,,	,,	,,	,,	,,	,,	,,	Aircraft gun, prototype in 1928, produced in 1931

Name of Weapon	Ammunition	Method of Operation	Method of Locking	Feed and Capacity	Cooling	Weight (lbs)	Rate of Fire (Rpm)	Muzzle Velocity ft/s	Remarks
Russian Guns (Cont.)									
Degtyarev DT	7.62mm X 54 R	Gas-piston	Projecting lugs	Flat drum 60	Air	20	500–600	2 770	Tank gun, prototype in 1929, produced in 1931
DP	7.62mm X 54 R	"	"	Flat drum 47	"	"	"	"	Modified Infantry gun with quick change barrel and return spring moved from under barrel
DT	7.62mm	"	"	Flat drum 60	"	"	"	"	Modified tank gun with return spring moved to rear of body as DPM
DS	7.62mm X 54 R	"	"	Belt 250	"	26.4	500–600 and 1 000–1200	2 650	Proposed new Medium MG. Appeared in the 1930s. Difficult to manufacture—never in service
DK	12.7mm	"	"	Belt 50	"	73½	550–600	2 763	Heavy MG appeared in 1934. Never adopted in quantity
D.Sh.K. 1938	12.7mm	"	"	Belt 50	"	73½	550–600	2 763	Designed by Degtyarev but rotating block feed by Shpagin. Limited production
(38–46)	12.7mm	"	"	"	"	"	"	"	Feed mechanism changed to Degtyarev type. Standard Russian AA gun in WW II. Later used in tanks and now in APCs
Degtyarev RP-46 "Company MG"	7.62mm X 54 R	Gas-piston	Projecting lugs	Belt 50 or Flat drum 47	Air	29	600–650	2 750	DP modified to take either belt or magazine. Heavy quick change barrel. Appeared in 1946.
RPD	7.62mm X39 M43	"	Projecting lugs but simplified	Belt 100	"	15½	650–750	2 400	Post War II design. Fixed barrel. Standard Soviet section gun from 1950–1965
Gatling (10 barrels)	4.2 line (approx. 10.6mm)	Hand cranked	Cam lock	Hopper	"	444	Optional		400 purchased in 1871 from Gatling Gun Co Hartford. Inspected by Gen Gorloff and known in Russia as Gorloff. Later manufactured at Tula.
Goryunov M43	7.62mm X 54 R	Gas-piston	Sideways tilting block	Belt 250	Air	32	500–700	2 620	Standard Russian MMG from 1943. Still in use. Central rear cocking handle
SGM	7.62 X 54 R	"	"	"	"	"	"	"	Fluted barrel. Adjustment for CHS. Cocking handle on right. Otherwise as M43.
SGT	7.62mm X 54 R	Gas-piston	Rotating bolt	Belt 200	"	"	"	"	Tank version of SGM
Kalashnikov PK GPMG	"	"	"	"	Air	21	750–1 000	2 800	PK is GPMG replacing SGM. PKS is sustained fire version. PKT is solenoid fired Tank version.
RPK	7.62mm X 39	"	"	Magazine 40 Drum 75	"	14	600	2 200	Uses same design as AK assault rifle. Fixed barrel. Now replaced the RPD assault LMG
KPV	14.5mm	Recoil	Rotating bolt head	Belt	"	108	600	3 280	Fires cartridge designed for A.Tk rifle. Designed by Vladimirov. Used as AA gun. Twin towed ZPU2 SP quadruple ZPU4. Now also used in Tks and APC's.

Russian Guns (Cont.)

Name of Weapon	Ammunition	Method of Operation	Method of Locking	Feed and Capacity	Cooling	Weight (lbs)	Rate of Fire (Rpm)	Muzzle Velocity ft/s	Remarks
Madsen Model 1903	7.62mm X 54 R 3 line (approx. 7.62mm)	Recoil	Hinged block	Magazine 20	Air	21	500-600	2 500	Danish gun used by Russian Cavalry in Russo-Japanese war 1904-5.
Maxim PM		Recoil-gas assisted	Toggle joint	Belt 250	Water	69 (1905) 44 (1910)	500 500	2 620 2 800	Bought from Maxim Gun Co. in 1890s. Manufactured at Tula in 1905. Improved in 1910. Manufactured at Slatoust-Vrzhumka
PV-1 (1920)	7.62mm X 54 R	"	"	"	Air	31.7	800	2 800	Aircraft gun. Light barrel casing and improved recoil.
M-T (Maxim-Tokarev)	7.62mm X 54 R	"	"	"	"	36	500-600	2 800	Shoulder stock and bipod. Used in Spanish Civil War and Russo-Finnish War
Maxim M-k (Maxim-Koleshnikov)	7.62mm X 54 R	Recoil-gas assisted	Toggle	Belt 250	Air	38	500-600	2 800	Shoulder stock and bipod. Tried in Spanish Civil War but not adopted
Esinunin	13mm	Recoil	"	Belt 50	Water		300		Esinunin was a designer at Tula. Only a few made.
NS 23	23mm	Recoil	Rotating bolt Head	Belt	Air	121	600-700	2 850	Gun designed by Nudelman. Feed designed by Suranov 1947. Based on 37mm model of 1943.
SHVAK	20mm	Gas-piston	Tilting block	Belt	Air	150	700-750	2 650	Aircraft gun Barrel length 65in. Improved feed based on Shkas. A few guns made in 12mm
Aircraft	20mm	"	"	"	"	88	700-750	2 600	Barrel length 51in. Also Tank use. SHVAK designed by Shpitalny and Vladimirov
SHKAS Model 33 Model 35 Model 36 Model 41	7.62mm (Special cartridge)	"		Belt into cage on gun	"	23½	1 800 2 000	2 430	Designed by Shpitalny and Komaritsky in 1933. Used throughout World War II and in Korea.
Vickers	7.62mm X 54 R	Recoil-gas assisted	Toggle joint	Belt 250	Water	41	500-600	2 800	Made by Colt 1914-1917
ZU 23	23mm	Gas-piston	Rising locking piece	Belt	Air	155	800-1000	2 850	Current AA gun also possibly for use in APCs

133

Index

ROGERIVS BACO,
Monachus in Anglia.
Astrologiae Chemiae et Mathe-
seos peritissimus.
Nat. A.1206. Den. A.1284.
Ex Collectione Friderici Roth-Scholtzii Norib.

1. Roger Bacon (1219–92) did not invent gunpowder, but was familiar with its properties and recorded how it was made in 1248.

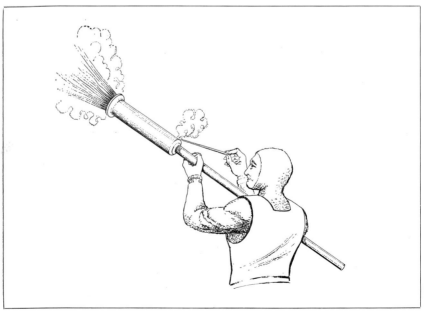

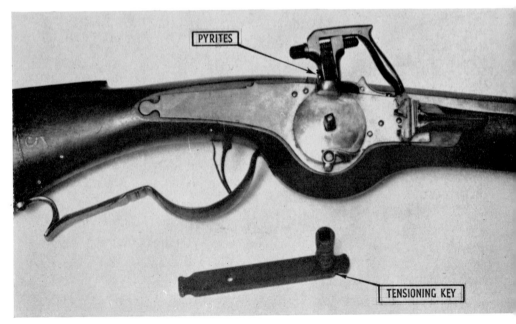

2. The Crecy bombard hurled a stone ball and was used in 1346.

3. The soldier muzzle loaded his powder, wad and ball and primed the touch hole of the 14th Century Cannon Lock. Ignition came from a hot ember and later a slow match burning at 2–3 inches an hour.

4. The Match Lock. 15th Century. The burning match was held in a serpentine and pulling the trigger moved the match to the priming pan.

5. The principle of the 16th Century Wheel-Lock was the same as the modern cigarette lighter. The spring, when released, rotated the knurled edge of the wheel against a flint and the sparks ignited the priming powder. It was expensive and difficult to repair.

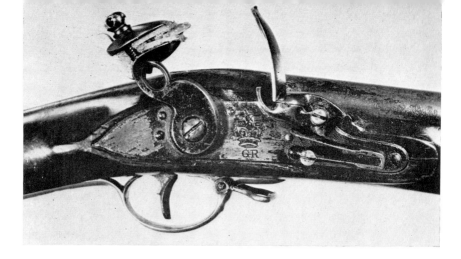

6. The Flint Lock. 17th Century. The flint was held in a jaw and when cocked the spring was compressed. The trigger released the spring, the flint struck the steel and the sparks ignited the powder.

7. The Organ Gun. 18th Century. This example was fired by flint lock and discharged 30 rifle calibre balls. It was presented by King Edward to the Royal United Services Institute, who later sold it. It is now in America.

8. Puckle's Gun of 1718 was not a machine gun but an early form of flintlock revolver. On March 31 1722, the London Journal reported that it was discharged 63 times in 7 minutes. It was supposed to fire round balls against Christians and square balls against Turks. It is now in the Tower of London.

9. Forsyth's Scent Bottle, 1807. Mercury fulminate was stored in one half, rotated over to fill the flash channel, rotated back to bring the firing pin under the hammer which then was released by the trigger. The flash went down the hollow spindle to ignite the gunpowder in the barrel.

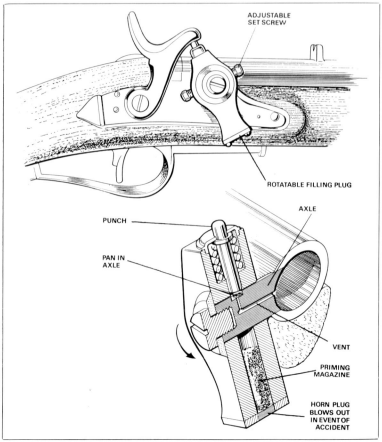

ADJUSTABLE
SET SCREW

ROTATABLE FILLING PLUG

PUNCH

AXLE

PAN IN
AXLE

VENT

PRIMING
MAGAZINE

HORN PLUG
BLOWS OUT
IN EVENT OF
ACCIDENT

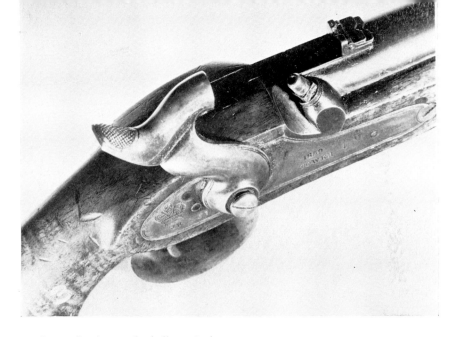

10. A cap, fitted over the hollow nipple, was crushed by the hammer and the flash travelled to the powder charge. This, the Percussion Lock, was a great advance because the weapon functioned in rain or wind.

11. Sir James Lillie's Battery Gun of 1857 was a 12 barrelled weapon, each barrel having its own revolving cylinder. There were more chambers in the bottom cylinders than the top. It could be controlled to fire all barrels simultaneously or in succession. It was never adopted and is now in the Rotunda Museum at Woolwich.

12. Dr. Gatling with Model 1893 Bulldog. Richard Jordan Gatling invented the first hand-operated rapid fire gun to achieve adoption. It was used during the American Civil War.

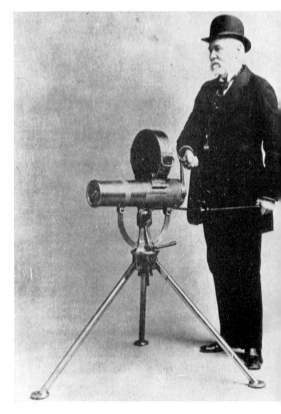

13. The Navy were far less conservative than the Army in Britain and used the .65in Gatling Gun on a pedestal mount shown here, in the foretops and with a wheeled carriage for shore parties.

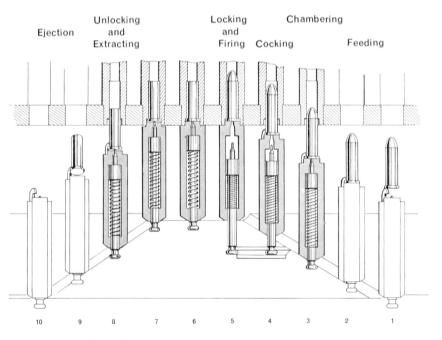

Ejection   Unlocking and Extracting   Locking and Firing   Cocking   Chambering   Feeding

10   9   8   7   6   5   4   3   2   1

15. The action of the Gatling Gun.

14. ◀ British Naval Brigade Clearing Streets of Alexandria with the Gatling Gun. Captain (later Admiral of the Fleet) Lord Fisher commanded the Naval Brigade during the riots of 1882. The sailors fired above the heads of the mob which dispersed at once.

16. Six barrel improved Gatling, on Infantry carriage belonging to the 3rd Battalion London Rifle Volunteers. Circa 1895.

17. Accles Gun. James Accles designed the Drum feed on the improved Gatling. He later came to England, improved the drive and feed arrangements on the Gatling gun and it was manufactured in Birmingham as the Accles Gun.

18. The ammunition of the Montigny Mitrailleuse was pre-loaded into the 37 holes in a steel plate which was inserted from the top when the breech was screwed back. A crank on the right allowed simultaneous or consecutive fire. Twelve plates could be loaded each minute.

19. The Battle of Gravelotte, 1870 was one of the few occasions when the Mitrailleuse was deployed as an Infantry weapon, forward, rather than as an artillery piece where the Prussian Artillery quickly neutralized it.

20. The Lowell Gun invented by De Witt Clinten Farrington of Lowell, Massachusetts in 1875, was an amazingly advanced design. It fired 50 000 rounds in $1\frac{1}{2}$ working days with only two stoppages when tested at the Annapolis Navy Yard.

21.◄ The Lowell Gun, showing feed and barrel arrangements. Only one barrel was used and when this became over-heated or a case jammed, another barrel was rotated into position in seconds.

23. The Nordanfelt action. ►

24. The Gardner twin barrelled gun on an overbank mounting. William Gardner of Toledo, Ohio, designed this gun. It was of .45 calibre. Tests in America were successful but produced no orders. The Royal Navy adopted it in 1884. ►

22▼ The 5 Barrelled .45 Naval Nordanfelt, designed by Heldge Palmcranz and marketed by Thorston Nordanfelt. The guns ranging from twin barrels to 12, were well made and reliable although in the 1880s the design was virtually obsolescent when first produced.

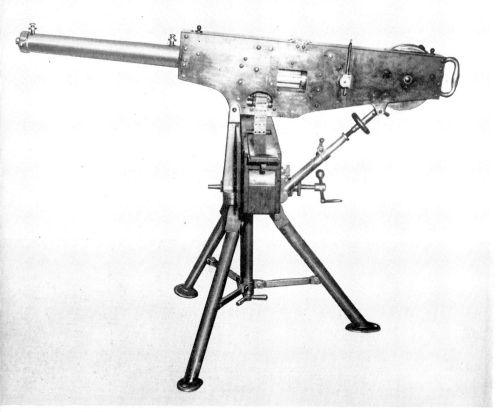

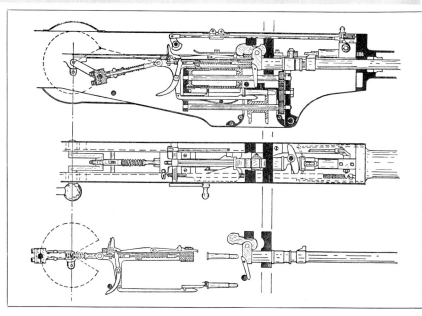

25. ◄ The "first" Maxim model was designed in 1883 and was quite different to the model later marketed. It was 4 ft 9 inches from muzzle to the rear of the casing and stood 3½ ft high. It had a variable rate of fire from 1 to 600 rounds a minute. Without water it weighed 60 lb.

26. The action of the "first" Maxim model. Note the hook device locking the breech block to the barrel and, in the middle drawing, the lever type accelerator. The gun resembles the Gardner in its use of a rotating crank, but the arc of rotation is limited. The bottom drawing shows the breech block to the rear and the feed and extraction systems.

27. ► Hiram Stevens Maxim and his Light Gun. This is said to be Maxim's favourite picture. It certainly shows the reduction in size over his first model and a great simplification.

28. ▼ The further gun is a standard light gun. In front of it is Maxim's demonstration gun which he carried in a small suitcase. It was a replica of the other gun but chambered for an early pistol cartridge—possibly from the pistol he designed himself. This gun is believed to be unique. It is held in the collection in the Pattern Room at the Royal Small Arms Factory, Enfield Lock and this collection, undoubtedly the best in this country, can be viewed by making an appointment through the Superintendent RSAF.

29. ◀ The Chinese envoy in London, Li Hung Chang, was a very colourful personality and very astute. When Maxim demonstrated the power of his Tree Chopper gun by cutting down a tree, Li Hung Chang asked the cost of firing the gun for one minute. He was told it was about thirty pounds sterling and remarked "That won't do for China. It is much too expensive".

30. ◀ The 1 pdr Maxim Pom-Pom was designed as an anti-torpedo boat gun for the Admiralty. As the Navy changed its mind the guns were sold to France who, in turn, sold them to the Boers. They produced great casualties amongst the British gunners and on many occasions neutralized our Maxim rifle calibre guns.

31. Lord Dundonald's Machine Gun Galloping Carriage. The Commanding Officers of the Volunteer Battalions bought the guns and carriages at their own expense.

32. Two light air-cooled Maxim automatic machine guns, 1896, at the Navy and Military Tournament, London. Mounted on a tricycle made for two, in such a way that the gun can be fired from the machine or separated and mounted on tripods. The gunners belong to the 2nd Battalion Tower Hamlet Volunteers while the escort belong to the 26th Battalion Middlesex Volunteers (Cyclists).

33. The Maxim Gun used by the Machine Gun Detachment of the King's Royal Rifles in India during the Chitral Campaign. Their devastating fire on the tribesmen's redoubt allowed the Infantry to capture the position with very small losses to themselves.

American Machine Guns

34. This experimental model of Browning's first machine gun proved that a gas operated gun was feasible by firing 16 shots a second. The cartridge was the black powder .44–40. A lot more work was needed before his gun was offered to Colt's Patent Firearm Corporation on November 22, 1890.

35. The Browning family outside their gunshop at Ogden, Utah. From left to right they are Sam, George, John, Matt and Ed Browning. The last figure is an unknown gunsmith.

36. John Moses Browning with the Colt model 95 machine gun. This gun was the first true machine gun—deriving its working energy from the pressure of the propellant gases —to be purchased by the United States. The U.S. Navy obtained 50 in 1897. They were used by the U.S. Marines with great success in Peking during the Boxer Uprising in 1900. The gun is known as the "potato-digger" because a swinging arm was forced down and back to a position vertically beneath the barrel. This prevented the firer lying prone behind the gun.

37. Mariner Browning demonstrating his uncle's 1901 recoil operated gun. John Browning decided recoil operation was preferable to gas operation and in 1901 he produced a recoil operated gun. It was further improved in 1910 and again in 1916 before being demonstrated at Congress Heights, February 27, 1917, where it was immediately proclaimed and adopted.

38. The Browning automatic rifle was demonstrated also at Congress Heights to the Press, Senators, Congressmen and Military Attachés. It became the American Light Machine Gun and was used in the Infantry squad until the introduction of the M60 GPMG in the late 50's.

39. The Marlin-Rockwell aircraft machine gun, model 1918, which followed and improved the Model 1917. Both came from the Colt 1895 model modified by Carl Swebilius who replaced the swinging arm by a gas piston under the barrel. This became the standard American aircraft machine gun and was the first gas operated gun to be synchronized.

40. The Marlin-Rockwell tank machine gun, model 1918. The introduction of the tank to the American Forces necessitated a new machine gun. The Marlin gun was successful but was not developed after the end of the war.

An infantry gun, which was basically the tank gun with the finning removed, was also produced but in small quantity.

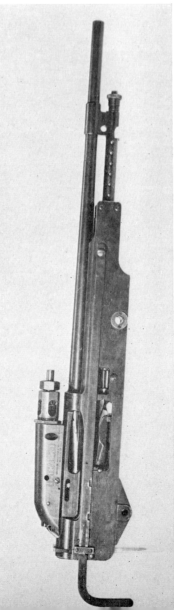

41. U.S. .5 M2 water-cooled machine gun. Manned by Free French soldiers, this gun guards a crossing of the Garigliano River in Italy, 1943.

42. U.S. 3rd Army Troops fighting in Coblenz on March 17, 1945, using Browning M1917A1 machine guns.

43. The CH-47A Chinook Helicopter, in Vietnam during 1966, carries a Browning .5 machine gun in the waist, a 20 mm gun firing forward as well as 2.75 inch rockets. All of these to attack ground targets.

44. ▲ Israeli Armoured Infantry with the M1919A4 Browning. This photograph was taken during the Six-Day War. The Israeli infantry mounted in armoured half tracks carrying 81 mm mortars and the Browning .30 machine gun were extremely mobile and swept round Egyptian positions to attack them from the rear.

45. ◄ On June 7, 1912 a Wright B Pusher piloted by Lt Milling engaged a ground target at the U.S. Army Experimental Flying Station, College Park, Washington. Capt. Chandler, the C.O. fired the Lewis gun, the first to be fired from an aircraft, and got 5 hits out of 47 rounds fired at a target 6ft × 7ft. The photograph shows Chandler but Milling was away when the photograph was taken and a substitute pilot took his place.

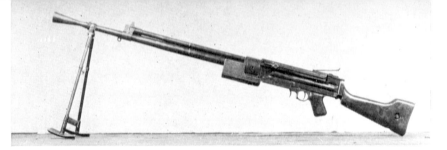

46. When Col Lewis failed to interest the U.S. Ordnance Board in his gun he went to Liège and produced guns of this type. Shortly afterwards BSA Birmingham took over manufacture.

47. The Lewis .303 LMG Mk 1 was produced initially because of the shortage of Vickers M.M.G.s but its light weight and mobility made it very suitable for employment in the front line and in 1915 Vickers guns were withdrawn from Infantry Battalions and Brigades. Four Lewis guns were issued per Battalion instead. By 1918 the scale of issue had

risen to 36 guns to each Battalion. It stayed in service with the Regular Army until replaced by the Bren in 1939.

48. The Lewis .303 Mk 2 aircraft machine gun was the most successful observer's gun of the First World War. Although used early on, firing forward mounted on the top of the biplane upper wing over the propeller arc, it was replaced by the Vickers which not only had a larger ammunition supply but could easily be synchronized to fire through the propeller.

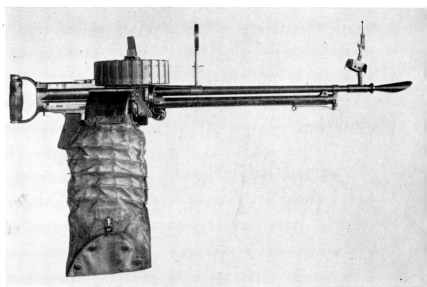

49. The Lewis .303 Mk 3 aircraft machine gun. The cowling and aluminium radial fins were not needed as the aircraft movement produced sufficient air cooling.

50. This gun, the Lewis .303 Mk 4 was issued as a ground LMG to the Home Guard in 1940. It was an adapted Mk 3 aircraft gun.

51. Lewis .303 Soley experimental. The Soley Arms Co. modified the Lewis Gun to take a box magazine. At the time this and their next gun, shown below, were evolved, the decision had been made to replace the Lewis gun by a lighter more modern design.

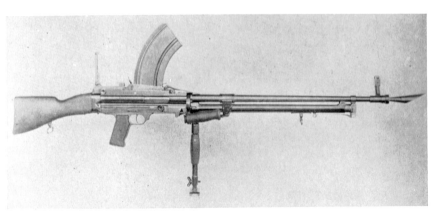

52. Lewis .303 Mk 4 modified by Soley. The clock-type Lewis return spring wound up by a rack cut on the underside of the piston extension, was replaced by a helical spring and the drum magazine by a box.

53. The Lewis .30 Model 1918 aircraft machine gun is shown with the 97 round drum and a muzzle booster to put up the rate of fire. This American gun was sent to this country after Dunkirk and was used by both regular and Home Guard units for anti-aircraft defence. A red line was painted on the gun to indicate that it took the .30–06 round and not .303.

54. After World War II the Americans had a development programme for a new infantry machine gun. The T44 7.62mm machine gun was a German FG 42 based weapon with a side feed arm taken from the German MG 42. It was a step in the development of the M60.

55. A GI carrying the M60 7.62mm machine gun in South Vietnam. The M60 replaced the BAR as a light machine gun and the Browning A4 as a sustained fire machine gun. It weighs 23lb and it is a composite of the German FG 42 bolt and the MG 42 feed.

56. The M60 7.62mm general purpose machine gun. The gas operating system incorporates a constant energy regulating system which removes the necessity for a manual regulator. The gas cylinder is attached to and removed with the barrel which also has a bipod permanently attached.

57◄ The M60c 7.62mm machine gun mounted on a British Sioux Helicopter. One such gun is mounted on each side with 650 rounds per gun. 9° elevation adjustment is available from inside the cockpit.

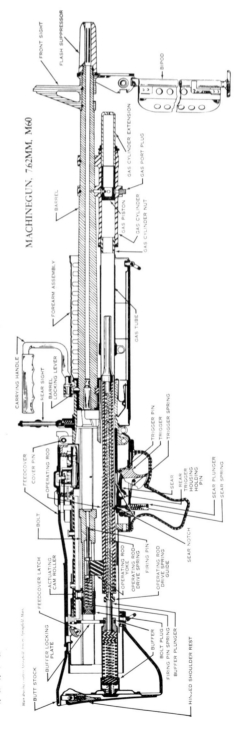

MACHINEGUN. 7.62MM, M60

173

58. The M73 7.62mm tank machine gun developed from the gun produced by Russell Robinson at the RSAF Enfield. This weapon produces the short in board length demanded of a tank machine gun. Its mechanism is complex and early models had a high stoppage rate. It is now standard in the M60 Tank.

59. Changing barrels on the M73. The gun can be adapted to feed from either side and to allow easy barrel change. In this photograph, taken from underneath the gun, the body has been swung to the left. The barrel casing is held in the armoured mantlet and the barrel can now readily be withdrawn and replaced.

60. The M85 .5 tank machine gun, the replacement for the Browning .5 M2, is now coming into service. It has a high rate of fire of 1 000 rounds a minute for anti-aircraft use and a slower rate of 400 for ground targets.

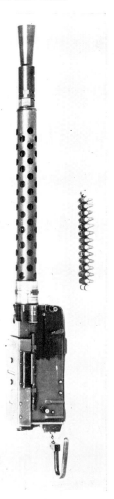

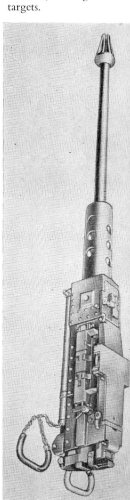

61. The 7.62mm Minigun. The Gatling principle of revolving barrels was utilized by the International General Electric Company of New York in an electrically powered high speed gun.

62. The 7.62mm Minigun mounted on a British Scout Helicopter. The main use of this gun is for the saturation of ground targets from the air. Firing at 6 000 rounds a minute the gun draws 120 amps from the battery.

63. The 7.62mm Minigun firing in a ground role. The ammunition supply is a critical factor in ground use.

64. The 20mm Vulcan M61 was the first of the revolving types produced by GEC. Here it is firing at 4 000 rounds per minute to test ammunition production at NWM.

65. ▶ For defence against air attack the Vulcan anti-aircraft system can be either towed or tracked. In each case it has on-mounting radar and fires at 4 000 rounds per minute to engage targets 1 000 metres away using full powered traverse to match supersonic target speeds.

66. The .223 Minigun. The latest of the series can fire up to 10 000 rounds a minute.

67. The Armalite AR-10 7.62mm LMG. Developed from Eugene Stoner's AR-10 rifle. This weapon will produce accurate fire which it can sustain at a continuous rate of about 40 rounds a minute. There are no barrel change facilities.

68. The Colt CAR-15. .223 (5.56mm) is a heavy barrelled belt fed adaptation of the Armalite AR-15 rifle. It again cannot produce more than 40 rounds a minute for a prolonged period without serious overheating.

69. The CMG-1 .223 tripod mounted medium machine gun. One of a series of Colt produced weapons based on common parts. Like all these families the lighter weapons are too heavy and the heavier weapons are not strong enough.

70. The Stoner 63AI .223 light machine gun. This was one of Eugene Stoner's productions for the Cadillac Gage Co. It is also now being produced in Holland by NWM, Kruithoorn. It is a good LMG, very accurate, easy to handle and change barrels, but originally somewhat under powered. Now this is put right it should be the best of the .223 LMGs.

71. The soldier of the post '70s. The Stoner 63AI is belt fed from the right so that the ammunition box does not hit the soldier's leg as he carries the gun by the carrying handle. With a 12½lb gun and lightweight ammunition the soldier should be less heavily laden in the future.

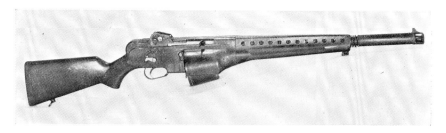

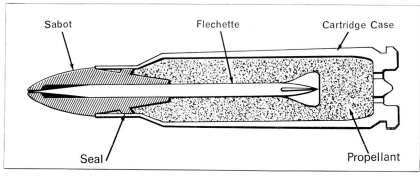

Sabot   Flechette   Cartridge Case

Seal   Propellant

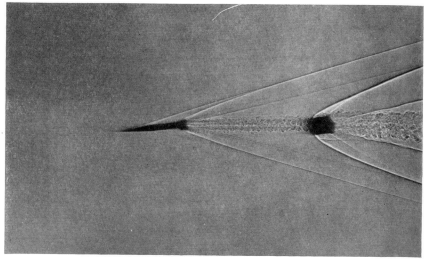

72. The AAI SPIW rifle carries 50 flechette rounds which it fires at 4 500 feet/second. It weighs, with ammunition, 8lbs and is the first generation weapon. With a bipod it has an LMG performance. SPIW stands for special purpose individual weapon.

73. The Flechette looks like a one inch steel nail with fins. It is surrounded in the cartridge case by the propellant and to enable the propellant force to be exerted over as large an area as possible, a sabot is fixed to the front of the flechette. This pulls the flechette down the smooth bore barrel and is stripped off at the muzzle leaving the flechette to travel on.

74. The Flechette in flight. The shock wave shows a high supersonic velocity. The flechette emerges at about 4 500ft/sec and at 400m this has dropped to about 3 000ft/sec.

The sabot is seen behind the flechette. Its poor shape and lack of density soon bring it to the ground.

British Machine Guns

75. Brig.-General N. R. McMahon DSO, psc—author of "Fire Tactics". Whilst Chief Instructor at the School of Infantry, Hythe, he urged the large scale employment of machine guns. His views were incorporated in the Field Service Regulations of both the British and German Armies. The indifference of the War Office to the value of the machine gun compelled him to concentrate on raising the standard of musketry and we sent to France in 1914, the finest infantry shots in the world. He was promoted to Brigadier-General in France in 1914 but was killed commanding the Royal Fusiliers before he could take over 10 Infantry Brigade.

76. The jacket of the Vickers .303 Mk 1 held seven pints of water which boiled after 3 minutes firing at 200 rounds a minute and evaporated thereafter at 1½ pints per 1 000 rounds. The steam passed through the steam tube and condenser hose to the condenser can and the water formed was poured back into the gun. The Vickers could fire at 10 000 rounds an hour for an indefinite period provided ammunition, water and spare barrels were available.

It was the finest medium machine gun in service anywhere and with Mk VIII Z ammunition it could neutralize targets with indirect fire—using a dial sight—up to 4 500 yards.

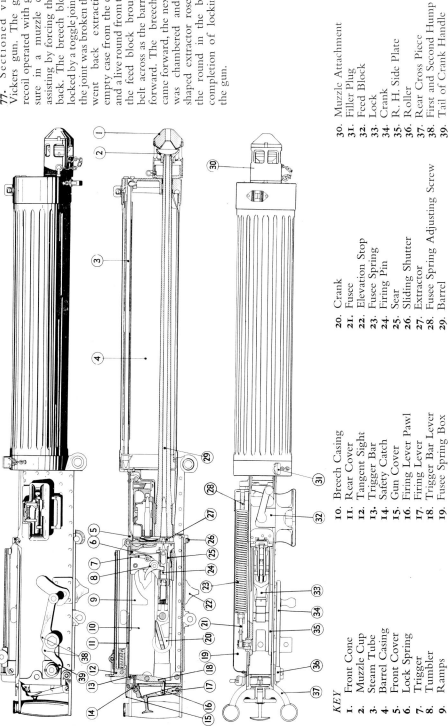

77. Sectioned view of Vickers gun. The gun was recoil operated with gas pressure in a muzzle chamber assisting by forcing the barrel back. The breech block was locked by a toggle joint. When the joint was broken the block went back extracting the empty case from the chamber and a live round from the belt; the feed block brought the belt across as the barrel went forward. The breech block came forward, the next round was chambered and the T shaped extractor rose to grip the round in the belt and completion of locking fired the gun.

KEY

1. Front Cone
2. Muzzle Cup
3. Steam Tube
4. Barrel Casing
5. Front Cover
6. Lock Spring
7. Trigger
8. Tumbler
9. Ramps
10. Breech Casing
11. Rear Cover
12. Tangent Sight
13. Trigger Bar
14. Safety Catch
15. Gun Cover
16. Firing Lever Pawl
17. Firing Lever
18. Trigger Bar Lever
19. Fusee Spring Box
20. Crank
21. Fusee
22. Elevation Stop
23. Fusee Spring
24. Firing Pin
25. Sear
26. Sliding Shutter
27. Extractor
28. Fusee Spring Adjusting Screw
29. Barrel
30. Muzzle Attachment
31. Filler Plug
32. Feed Block
33. Lock
34. Crank
35. R. H. Side Plate
36. Roller
37. Rear Cross Piece
38. First and Second Hump
39. Tail of Crank Handle

78. Vickers .303 Mk 1 in action. In both World Wars the Vickers was employed in every theatre of operation. Here Commandos are giving supporting fire across the Rhine whilst 1 Commando Brigade mount a night assault crossing. They captured Wesel at 2 a.m., March 24, 1945, killing the German Commander, Major-General Deutsch and taking 350 prisoners.

79. Vickers .303 Mk 1* was modified by opening the front cap, cutting louvres in the jacket and altering the spade grips. This was the first allied gun firing between the propeller blades using the Constantinesco synchronizing gear.

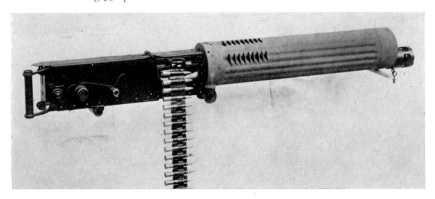

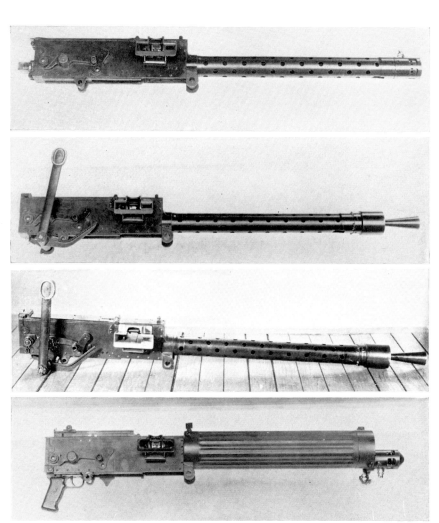

80. Vickers .303 Mk 2 superseded the Mk 1* as an aircraft gun.

81. The barrel casing of the Vickers .303 Mk 2* was similar to the Mk 2; a long flash hider, was added, and the cocking lever enabled the pilot to clear a stoppage in flight.

82. Vickers .303 Mk 3 was an improved aircraft gun.

83. Vickers .303 Mk 4 (prototype). The first, experimental, Armoured Fighting Vehicle machine gun.

FACING PAGE
84. Vickers .303 Mk 4b. The Mk 4a was never in unit service. The 4a and 4b were factory modified Mk 1 guns with dovetail mounting plates.

85. Vickers .303 Mk 5, the final version of the fixed, forward firing, aircraft machine gun.

86. Vickers .303 Mk 6, an AFV gun developed from the Mk 4b with a stronger dovetail. Note the corrugated casing.

87. Vickers .303 Mk 7. The vehicle cooling system was connected to the gun. This example could be dismounted and used, in emergency, in a ground role. Note the plain casing.

88. Vickers rifle calibre machine gun—class 'A' was a Vickers commercial model with an aluminium sleeve over the air-cooled barrel. The body sideplates extend forward to the muzzle. Single shot came from the bottom trigger, full auto from the top. It never came into British Service.

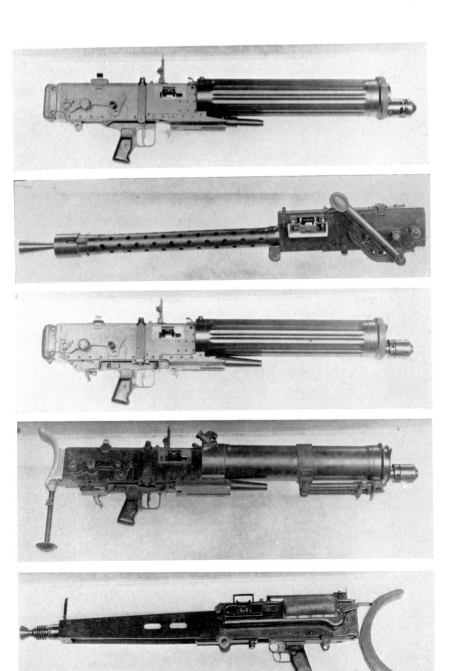

89. Vickers rifle calibre machine gun—class 'A' variant. The spade grips, different sights and muzzle attachment all vary from the standard class 'A' gun.

90. Czech Vickers made for the Greek Air Force. This is a variant on the Vickers commercial class 'F' gun with a thinner jacket and non-standard cocking lever.

91. The Vickers .5 Mk 1 was built as a prototype only. It was a scaled up .303 Mk 1 and like all Vickers .5 machine guns, had no muzzle assistance from the emerging gases.

92. Vickers .5 Mk 2. The first production gun. Used by the Army.

93. Vickers .5 Mk 3, used only by the Navy. It had a large flash hider and a cocking lanyard. It had arrangements for remote control. Seen here in a multiple pom-pom mounting on a frigate.

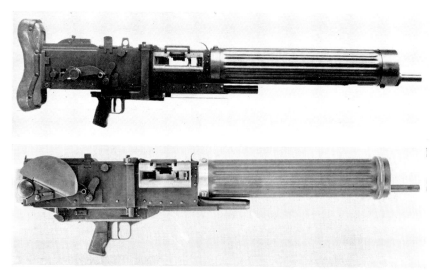

94. Vickers .5 Mk 4, an AFV gun. Distinguished at first glance by the cartridge ejector tube being part of the body and separate from the trigger grip.

95. Vickers .5 Mk 5, the final form of the tank machine gun.

96. Vickers .5 aircraft machine gun. The body sideplates extend forward to the muzzle. The gun was remotely controlled and synchronised.

97. Vickers-Berthier .303 LMG Mk 3 was made at the Ishapur Rifle Factory, India, and was the standard gun for the Indian Army.

98. Vickers-Berthier .303 LMG Mk 2, lightened for jungle warfare. This was a prototype gun modified by Vickers at Crayford at the request of the Indian Government. Like the Mk 1 it had a different gas plug and was 3lbs lighter than the standard gun, but was never adopted for service.

99. Vickers class 'D' .5 high velocity gun, developed with a special cartridge as an Anti-Aircraft gun. It is seen here mounted on a railway truck in the Mesopotamia campaign in 1916.

100. Experimental twin heavy barrel Vickers .303 tank machine gun. This gun was a private venture. It had two barrels side by side. When one was overheated the other was rotated into position in a manner reminiscent of the Lowell machine gun (21). It was gas operated. (The version shown lacks the backplate.)

101. Charlton LMG .303. The New Zealand Army modified a S.M.L.E. No. 1 rifle during World War I to produce a LMG. A gas piston was connected to a cam plate in which rested the bolt. It was heavy, cumbersome, susceptible to dirt, and was never adopted.

102. The Czechoslovakian Zb26 LMG 7.92mm designed by Vaclav Holek at Brno. This LMG was reported on, very favourably, by the British Military Attaché at Prague in 1929. It was tested against the Vickers-Berthier and the Danish Madsen (Fig 212) and did very well.

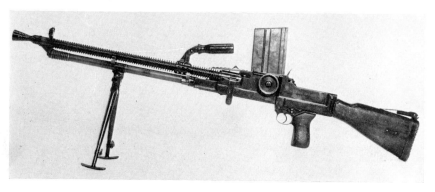

103. Czechoslovakian Zb30 LMG. (.303 Experimental). The next model from Brno was chambered in .303 instead of 7.92mm and sent to Enfield for evaluation.

104. Czechoslovakian Vz33 LMG. (.303 Experimental). The trials revealed that more power was required and so the gas port was brought nearer the breech face. The butt shape was also changed.

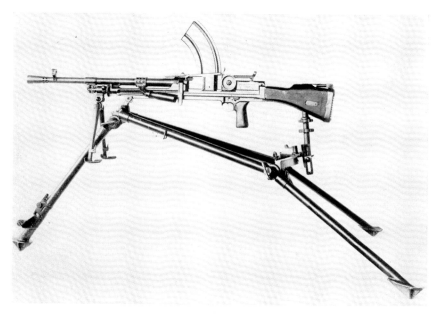

105. Czechoslovakian Vz34 LMG (.303 Experimental). The gas port position was finalised, the barrel finning removed and further trials conducted.

106. Czechoslovakian ZGB LMG .303. The Brno factory buffered the body, modified the gas cylinder and this became the final pattern for the Bren LMG.

107. German troops in France 1940 with the Zb30 LMG in 7.92mm. The Germans took over and continued production at Brno when they invaded Czechoslovakia in 1938. Thus both British and,. to a lesser extent the Germans, had basically the same gun.

FACING PAGE

108. Bren LMG Mk 1 .303, distinguished by the long barrel, drum aperture tangent backsight and shoulder strap. It also had a handle below the butt (**109**).

109. Bren LMG Mk 1 .303 with 200 round high speed magazine, intended for use against aircraft.

110. The barrel of the Bren LMG Mk 2 .303 was shortened and the gun lightened. A leaf rear sight was fitted. The bipod legs could not be adjusted for length. The handle under the butt was removed.

111. The barrel of the Bren LMG Mk 3 .303 was further shortened.

112. The Bren LMG was used by all British Forces, the Free French, the Poles, the Indian Army and, here, by the Australians serving under McArthur in New Guinea.

195

113. The Bren LMG L4 7.62mm. When the NATO 7.62mm round was adopted the Mk 3 Bren was converted and is now issued to all units except infantry and tanks.

114. BESA Mk III and Mk III*—7.92mm. The Mk I was identical to the Czech model 53. The Mk II embodied changes to ease manufacture. The Mk III and III* had only one rate of fire—450 rpm. BSA made 60 000 Mk II and III guns.

115.▶Czech Zb model 53—1937 7.92mm, shown here with Biafran troops in the war against Nigeria. The gun was taken by Britain in 1938 as a 7.92mm tank machine gun and was in service until the end of the war. It fired at either 450 or 750 rounds/minute.

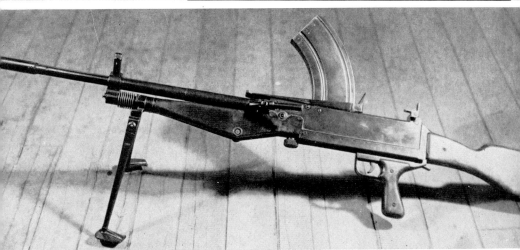

116. The BESA 15mm Mk 1 was taken straight from the Zb60. It was used in British armoured cars. Only 3 000 were made. Later production models had no holes in the body side plates.

117. BESAL LMG .303 Mk 1. This gun was designed by Harry Faulkoner of BSA for production if Enfield was bombed and Bren production stopped. It cocked like a Bren gun.

118. The BESAL LMG .303 Mk 2 cocked like a BESA, i.e. the pistol grip was pushed forward and then, the catch released, on pulling back, the bolt and piston were drawn to the rear. The BESAL—or Faulkoner as it was later named—never came into service.

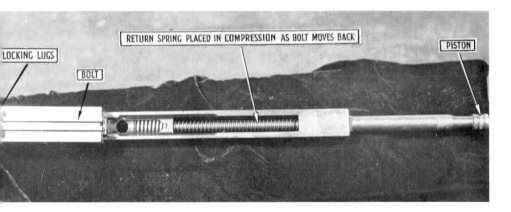

LOCKING LUGS   BOLT   RETURN SPRING PLACED IN COMPRESSION AS BOLT MOVES BACK   PISTON

119. BESAL—bolt, piston and return spring.
The gun was simple, robust and reliable. It
was cheap and would have been simple to
produce in quantity.

120. Beardmore-Farquhar .303 aircraft
machine gun, designed by Colonel Mowbray Gore Farquhar and manufactured
in Birmingham by Beardmore. It was
light and of unconventional design using
springs instead of direct piston action. The
RAF tested it—successfully—in 1919. With
77 rounds it weighed only 16½lb. It came
too late for the First World War and too
soon for the Second. It was also tested in
1921 at Enfield as a ground gun.

121. BSA .5 observer's gun. This fired at
the very slow rate of 400rpm and had only
37 rounds in a drum magazine. It was not—
as often believed—a .5 Lewis but was recoil
operated.

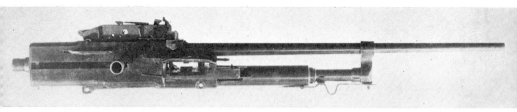

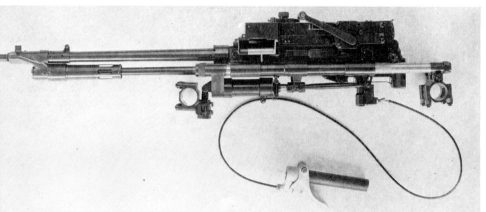

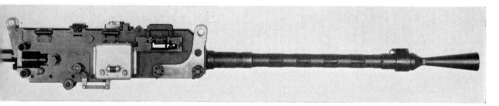

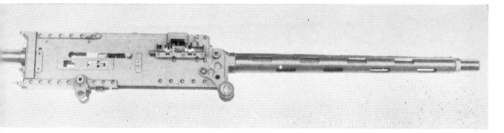

122. Darne .303 aircraft machine gun. A trial held at Martlesham Heath in 1935 settled the gun for the next generation of fighters. This French gun was one contender. It had many stoppages.

123. Gebauer .303 aircraft machine gun. This gun was designed by Kirali and made by Danuvia in Hungary. It was the fastest firing machine gun ever made. In its trial it averaged 2 000 rounds a minute. It was unreliable and very complex.

124. Vickers central action .303 machine gun. The coil return spring was located behind the lock. Otherwise a faster firing Vickers gun of conventional pattern. It was good but not good enough.

125. Although marketed by Colt's Patent Firearms Corp., the Colt MG40 .303 machine gun was the Browning gun later known as the 30 cal M2. It fired at 1 200rpm and was completely reliable in all attitudes. It was accepted by the RAF.

126. The original Mk 1 .303 air S machine gun was made in U.S.A. for the RAF, and modified in U.K. production versions before the Battle of Britain. It could be either left or right hand feed.

127. The Browning Mk 2 .303 aircraft machine gun was the Battle of Britain Gun. U.K. manufactured by BSA. The RAF success in 1940 owed much to this gun.

128. When 12 of these guns were mounted in the Hurricane 2b, each firing at 1 200 rounds a minute, the aircraft delivered 360lbs of bullets each minute.

 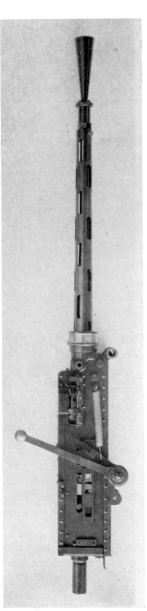 

129. The RAF tested the best guns available for use as an Observer's Gun. The French Darne observer's gun model 29 .303 was basically the same gun as that tried as a fixed gun.

130. The French Air Force used the Hotchkiss observer's gun and it was tested at Martlesham Heath in .303 but was not considered to be sufficiently reliable.

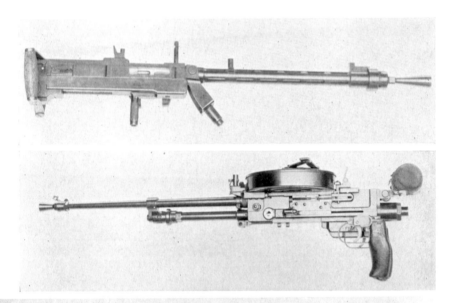

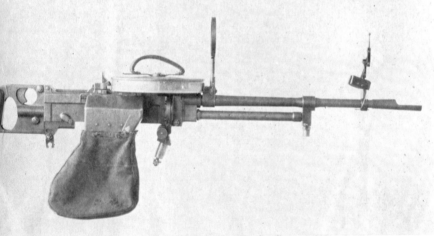

131. Designed by Aimo Lahti of the Finnish State Rifle Factory, the Lahti observer's gun .303 was a modified version of the Suomi L/S 26–32 recoil operated infantry LMG. It did not meet the RAF requirements. It had a flat 75 round drum magazine and fired at 500rpm.

132. Adams-Wilmot observer's gun .303. This gun was marketed by BSA. It was a gas operated gun weighing 20¼lbs with either a 60 or 90 round drum. The firing pin broke early in the trial and when this was replaced it had numerous feed stoppages. It was too unreliable to complete the tests.

133. The action of this gun, the Vickers gas operated machine gun .303 was basically that of the Vickers Berthier. The bolt and piston were chrome plated. The gun fired at 900–1000 rounds a minute, was reliable in all attitudes and was adopted by the RAF. The advent of the power operated turret curtailed its employment since belt fed Brownings could be used. The No 1 and No 3 Mk 1 guns were air service. The No 2 and No 4 guns were ground service.

They were used by the Long Range Desert Group mounted in pairs on jeeps as a dual purpose ground and anti-aircraft gun.

134. The Rolls-Royce .5 aircraft machine gun was developed initially in 1941 to fire the .5 Browning ammunition. The barrel was six inches shorter than the Browning. The system of recoil operation was used, with projecting lugs, locking very similarly to Degtyarev's design in the Russian DP. An oil buffer was fitted. After trials at Pendine, it was decided to re-chamber for the Boys .55 Anti-tank rifle ammunition. At this stage the Ministry of Aircraft Production vetoed the project. The body of the gun was made of a Rolls-Royce hiduminium alloy. The gun is now in the Pattern Room, RSAF Enfield.

135. Russel Robinson .5 tank machine gun. This Australian designer came to Enfield in the late '40s and produced prototypes of a recoil operated sliding block machine gun, rammer fed with the empty case extracted by a lever arm which folded under the barrel line and held the case head forwards for ejection. The British did not use his design and he went to America where it played a part in the design of the U.S. M73 7.62mm tank machine gun.

136. Enfield experimental 7.92mm LMG. EM1. When the EM2 rifle was introduced using the "bull-pup" configuration work was carried out on a similar design for a LMG. Preliminary trials were based on the German FG-42 design but the magazine was placed behind the trigger group and the working parts—bolt and gas piston—came back into the butt. It was designed, like the EM2, by Jansen.

137. The TADEN .280 sustained fire machine gun (prototype), designed by Lt Col Turpin, a Vickers designer, at Enfield. This gun could have been the British General Purpose Machine Gun if the .280 Mk 1z round had been adopted in 1950. It is basically a utilisation of the Bren action operating a belt feed. It had a strong action and could lift 10ft of belted ammunition. Its maximum effective range was about 1 800 yards.

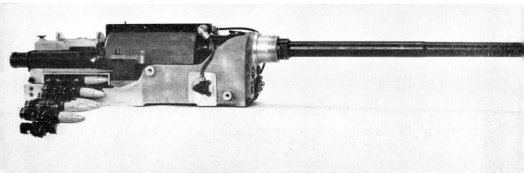

138. ADEN 30mm aircraft gun. The short engagement time and better aircraft protection led to the development of a large calibre fast firing revolver gun for the RAF developed from the German Mauser 213. It is also suitable for air-to-ground attack where the high speed of the aircraft gives added velocity to the shell.

139. BSA 7.62mm GPMG prototype). When the 7.62mm NATO round was adopted in 1952 this gun was developed by BSA from a Bren gun, to produce sustained belt fed fire. It was a very neat conversion and the feed drive from the piston was very efficient.

140. BSA 7.62mm GPMG—feed arrangement. The shaft on the right (indicated in the picture) is rotated by the piston as it comes back and this in turn is connected to the feed pawl which pulls the belt through the gun from the right. When the gas piston goes forward the feed pawl springs over the belt and grips the next round to be fed up. The belt stop pawls are mounted on the top cover.

141. XIIE4 7.62 GPMG (experimental). The Design & Development Department at the RSAF came up with this version of the 7.62mm GPMG. The feed arrangements were not so good as the BSA. The vertical shaft seen just behind the belted rounds was rotated by the piston and operated the feed pawl. There was a lot of friction in this drive and this resulted in a loss of power. The gun was tested in competition with the U.S.A. M60 (*see Fig* **55**), the French AA 52 (*Fig* **166**) the Madsen Saetter (*Fig* **236**), the SIG 510–2 and the FN MAG (*Fig* **142**). The FN gun was undoubtedly the best although the XIIE4 which had a longer barrel and sight base was extremely accurate.

142. M. Vervier of FN and the MAG 7.62mm GPMG. M. Vervier, the Chief Designer, and M. Lalou, Chairman of Fabrique Nationale d'Armes de Guerre, Liège, produced and marketed the MAG — Mitrailleuse à Gaz — which was a very reliable and accurate machine gun. Twenty-five countries in addition to the U.K. have purchased this gun, including Argentina, Cuba, India, Israel, New Zealand, Holland, South Africa and Sweden (6.5mm).

143. MAG 7.62mm GPMG on Belgian parachutable infantry car. This little car gives Belgian parachutists the mobility to exploit their fire power.

144. ▶ Detail of the British L7A1 7.62mm GPMG. The gun is gas operated, the locking system is a dropping link, it fires at 750–1 000 rpm and ranges out to 2 000m. It is reliable, sturdy and weighs 23½lb which when carried in the Infantry section is somewhat heavy. It has been in service since 1962.

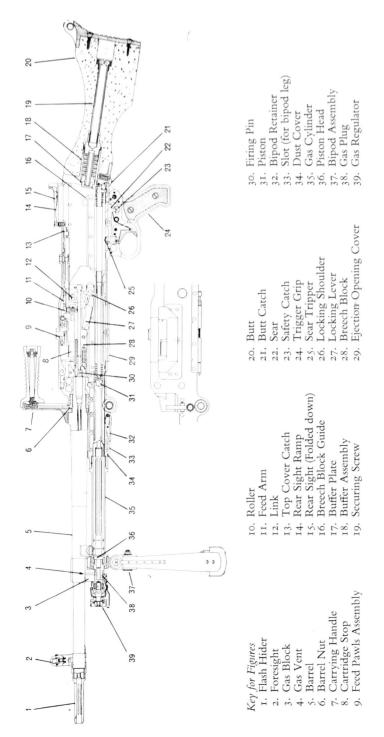

Key for Figures

1. Flash Hider
2. Foresight
3. Gas Block
4. Gas Vent
5. Barrel
6. Barrel Nut
7. Carrying Handle
8. Cartridge Stop
9. Feed Pawls Assembly
10. Roller
11. Feed Arm
12. Link
13. Top Cover Catch
14. Rear Sight Ramp
15. Rear Sight (Folded down)
16. Breech Block Guide
17. Buffer Plate
18. Buffer Assembly
19. Securing Screw
20. Butt
21. Butt Catch
22. Sear
23. Safety Catch
24. Trigger Grip
25. Sear Tripper
26. Locking Shoulder
27. Locking Lever
28. Breech Block
29. Ejection Opening Cover
30. Firing Pin
31. Piston
32. Bipod Retainer
33. Slot (for bipod leg)
34. Dust Cover
35. Gas Cylinder
36. Piston Head
37. Bipod Assembly
38. Gas Plug
39. Gas Regulator

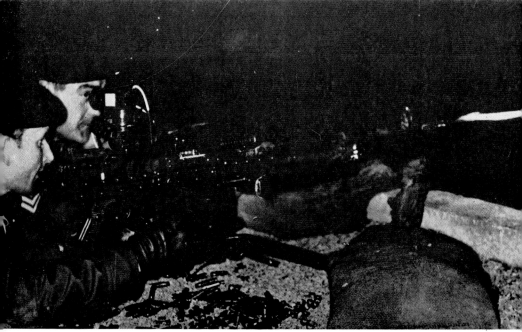

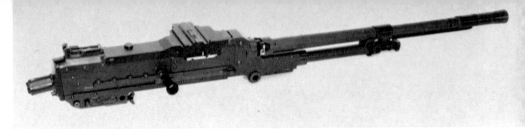

145. L7A1 7.62mm GPMG in the sustained fire role. Each Infantry Company HQ holds conversion kits consisting of tripod, spare barrels and dial sight to enable selected section weapons to be used in the sustained fire role. Although unable to produce the volume of fire of the old water-cooled Vickers .303 Mk 1, it is a very effective weapon.

146. L7A1 7.62mm GPMG firing at night. The No 1 is using an Infra-red night sight and firing the gun with his left hand. The No 2 is lying behind the gun.

147. L8 7.62mm tank machine gun. The L7A1 gas regulator discharges fumes to the atmosphere and so the L8 has a different, three position, regulator and a tube fitted from the regulator to carry any fumes to the muzzle gases. The gun has a feed pawl depressor on the top cover plate which allows removal of the belt without lifting the top cover plate.

The gun is co-axially mounted with the main armament and so has no sights.

148. Changing the barrel of the L8 7.62mm tank machine gun. With all gas operated guns the barrel must go forward on removal to clear it from the gas cylinder. In the Chieftain tank the entire gun is withdrawn to allow the barrel to be changed. There is no carrying handle on the L8 gun barrel so the hot barrel requires gloves.

149. L37 7.62mm tank machine gun. Where as the L8 is co-axially mounted with the the main armament, the L37 is the Commander's flexible gun. This photograph shows the conversion kit to change the L8 gun to the L37. Note the gun can have either the L7 gun barrel or the L8 gun barrel.

150. L37 7.62mm tank machine gun with L8 barrel. This would be used from the Commander's position in the top of the turret.

151. L37 7.62mm tank machine gun with L7 barrel. Here the gun would be deployed outside the tank—perhaps to defend a laager at night. Notice the carrying handle and the body with the feed pawl depressors.

152. The L20 7.62mm helicopter machine gun has the L7 body, L8 gas system with the L7 barrel and arrangements for remote control.

153. The RARDEN 30mm cannon. This gun is designed principally to destroy enemy Armoured Personnel Carriers at a sufficient range (1 000m) for mortars and artillery to deal with the enemy infantry before they can close with our troops. It is a long recoil operated gun with a self-loading action firing HE or Armour Piercing Discarding Sabot rounds at high velocity with great accuracy.

154. RARDEN 30mm mounted on AFV 432. The Infantry have now a means of defeating enemy APCs before they get close enough for their numerical superiority to be overwhelming.

155. RARDEN 30mm mounted on FOX. This Combat Vehicle Reconnaissance is primarily an information gathering and reporting vehicle but there will be times when it will be forced to fight for its information or be employed as part of a defensive screen. Then the RARDEN 30mm with its great hitting power will be invaluable.

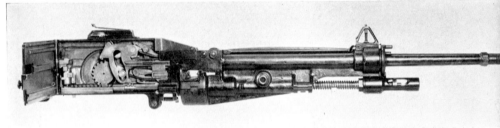

156. Hotchkiss 37mm gun. Designed by Benjamin Hotchkiss in 1871. It was later an anti-torpedo boat gun. Over 10 000 were produced at St. Denis, Paris and by William Armstrong & Co. at Elswick. Used by the navies of France, Belgium, Britain, Holland, Italy, Russia and U.S.A.

French Machine Guns

157. St. Etienne 8mm machine gun. Produced by the Arsenal of that name in 1907. The piston went *forward* when the gun fired. Attached was a spring loaded rod and rack. The rack rotated the reversing spur wheel which forced the breech block backwards. The spring drove the piston back and the rack and gear drove the block forward. This "gimmicky" arrangement gave a lot of stoppages.

215

158. Indian troops with Hotchkiss .303 LMG Mk 1 in France 1916. This gun was adopted in the U.S.A. as the Benét-Mercié in 1909. It was also the French model 1908. Adopted in the British Army on May 18, 1916 it remained in the Indian Army until the early 1930's.

160. ▲ Hotchkiss model 1914 in action with French troops 1915. This strip fed 8mm gun was the main French medium machine gun 1914–1918. It was also bought by the American Forces in 8mm and .30–06.

159. American troops with the French Chauchat LMG. Alsace 1918. The semi-circular magazine was used with the French 8mm Lebel cartridge. A most unreliable, long recoil operated weapon, the Americans bought tens of thousands of them.

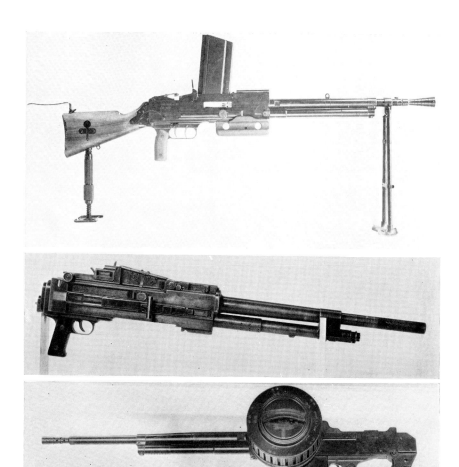

161. The Chatelleraut LMG 7.5mm 1924/29 model was the service version of the gun invented in 1921. It had a history of accidents and explosions in development. Front trigger was single shot, rear trigger automatic fire. It was used by French troops in 1940, and also saw service in Indo–China and Algeria.

162. Chatelleraut tank machine gun 7.5mm 1931 model. The feed on this gun was usually a drum on the right hand side but later versions had a top mounted box magazine which held 20 rounds.

163. Chatelleraut observer's aircraft machine gun 7.5mm model 1931. Like the Fortress model used in static defences this gun had the drum feed on the left.

218

164. Chatelleraut fixed aircraft machine gun 7.5mm model 1934. The 1931 model was improved to produce a high rate of fire. This was also drum fed but the 1939 model which was a further development, was belt fed.

165. The Hotchkiss aircraft machine gun 13.2mm. The French, generally, pioneered the use of larger calibre aircraft machine guns in the '30s. This gun—with a strip feed—was adopted by the Japanese as a ground anti-aircraft gun.

166. The action of the AA-52 GPMG 7.5mm gun is shown in diagram i. The French made some of these models in 7.62mm NATO for their forces working with that organisation but the 7.5mm model was the more usual. This delayed blowback system is very critical of cartridge head space adjustment and even in a new gun quickly develops bulged cases (*see Fig* **167**). Blown cases are not uncommon.

167. A fired cartridge case from an AA-52 GPMG. Note the bulge where the extractor groove in the chamber allowed expansion. The marks on the neck are caused by gas wash and deformation caused by the fluted chamber which is used to allow ready extraction.

168. Kaiser Wilhelm was very interested in the Machine Gun. In 1887 he came—as Crown Prince William of Prussia—to Queen Victoria's first Jubilee. He visited his cousin serving in the 10th Hussars at Hounslow. The CO, Lt Col Liddel, had purchased at his own expense a galloping carriage for the Nordenfelt pulled by two horses. The Emperor ordered a similar gun and carriage to be sent to Germany. Colonel Liddel sent one of his machine gunners to Potsdam to train German gunners in the working of the gun. (From a *History of the 10th Hussars*.)

The Kaiser urged upon the General Staff the necessity of buying the Maxim gun, but not until the reports came in from the attaché with the Japanese forces in the Russo-Japanese War of 1904 did the Germans start equipping with this gun in quantity.

German Machine Guns

169. A Maxim 7.92mm model 1908 on sledge mounting. It was drawn in action by two men. 15 000 rounds were supplied for each gun. The detachment was four men. It could be fired by a man lying, kneeling, sitting or standing.

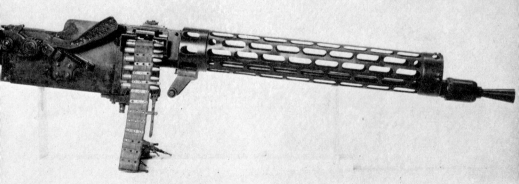

170. The Maxim 7.92 model 1908 in action. "Positions protected by barbed wire and defended by well served machine guns disposed in depth could not be taken even by the most resolute infantry and the casualty lists of the Somme and Paschendaele bear witness to the price paid for such failure". (Lt Col G. Hutcheson, O.C. 33 Machine Gun Company.) On the first day of the British Somme offensive—July 1, 1916 —our casualties mainly due to machine guns were 57 000. By the end of that battle they reached 419 654—author.

171. The Maxim 7.92mm aircraft machine gun. With the casing lightened and the gun air-cooled and synchronised it was very efficient.

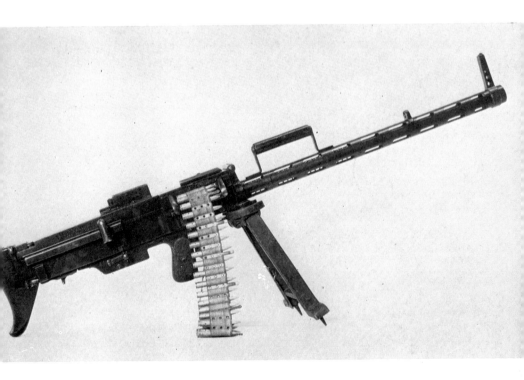

175▲ Bergman 7.92mm machine gun model 1915. This was a short recoil operated gun with a belt drum on the right hand side. It weighed 36lb and fired, cyclic, 800rpm. Although lighter and sturdily constructed it never replaced the 08–15 Maxim.

FACING PAGE

172. The Parabellum 7.92mm aircraft machine gun model 13. Karl Heineman of D.W.M. produced a lightweight, air-cooled version of the Maxim firing 700 rounds each minute. The toggle joint broke upwards like the Vickers. It was given priority as an aircraft gun although its light weight of 22lbs would have made it very suitable for the ground role.

173. This, the Gast 7.92mm twin barrelled aircraft machine gun, worked on the principle that the recoil of one barrel provided the energy for loading, chambering and firing the other. It had a rate of fire of 1 600 rounds a minute and weighed 60lbs. It was first demonstrated on August 22, 1917, but although manufacture started at once it was not in service when the war ended.

174. The Maxim 7.92mm machine gun model 08–15, a lightweight shoulder controlled Maxim with a 50 round belt container, was produced in 1915. It weighed 38lb with its water but had no steam tube or provision for condenser cans. It was used extensively throughout World War I with great success.

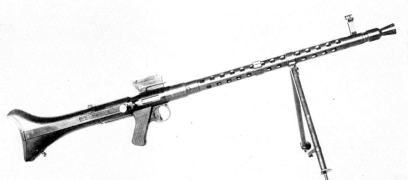

176. Derived from the Dreyse model 1915, improved in 1918, this gun, the MG-13. 7.92mm was adopted by the German Army in the early '30s. It fired 750rpm. When withdrawn from service in 1937 it was sold to Portugal and Spain.

177. Solothurn MG-30 7.92mm. The Swiss firm of Solothurn became a subsidiary of Rheinmetall in 1929. The MG-30 fired single shot from pressure on the top half of the trigger and full auto from the bottom. Taken by Hungary as the M31 and Austria as the M30 in 8mm.

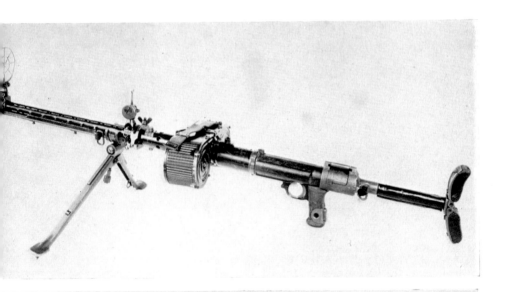

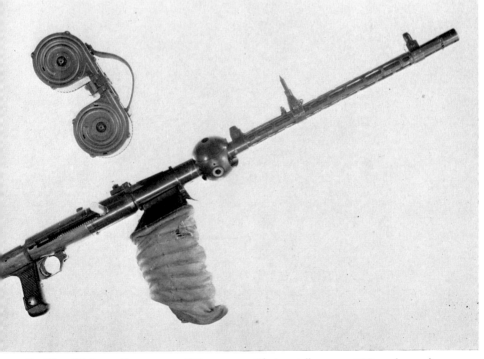

178. The Rheinmetall 7.92mm MG-15 ground role which used the locking ring introduced by Louis Stange in the MG 30 (*Fig* **177**). In the ground role it used the double, saddle, drum holding 75 rounds. It fired at 800rpm.

179. Rheinmetall 7.92mm MG-15 observer's gun. The aircraft version fired at 1 000rpm when fired from a rigid mounting and 800 when used on a flexible mount.

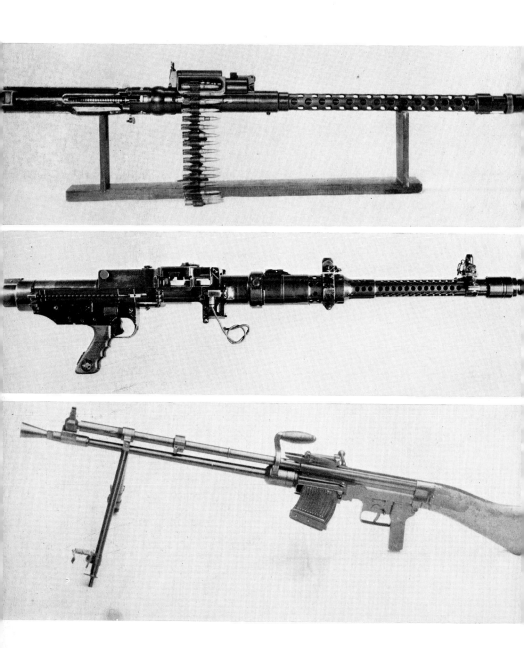

180. Rheinmetall 7.92mm MG-17 aircraft gun. The MG-15 was modified to fire from a closed breech, which is a necessity for synchronising, and a sprocket feed fitted. It could be re-cocked in flight by compressed air.

181. The Rheinmetall-Borsig 12.7mm MG-131 aircraft gun. In January 1936 Rheinmetall took over the bankrupt Borsig firm. The belt fed 131 weighed 40lbs and fired its .5 bullet at 2 560ft/s. Electrically fired, a pair were fitted to the power operated turret of the Dornier 217E. Fixed guns were electrically cocked, free guns were hand cocked.

182. Initially a Swedish gun, the Knorr-Bremse 7.92mm light machine gun was manufactured in 1935 by the Knorr-Bremse firm at Lichtenberg. The German Army did not adopt the gun but it was sold to Finland who used it against the Russians in the Battles of the Lakes, 1940.

183. ▼ German parachutists in Holland May 10, 1940 with the MG-34. The first genuine GPMG, the Mauser MG-34 was bipod mounted in the Infantry Section or tripod mounted for sustained fire. The rotating bolt head locking is ascribed to Louis Stange. It can either be belt fed or take the 75 round saddle drum. It was not suited for mass production although it was used throughout World War II.

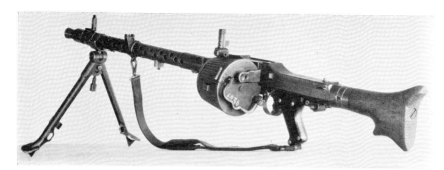

184. The Mauser MG-34 7.92mm machine gun belt fed was also the standard tank gun in World War II. It was recoil operated and the body rotated to one side to allow a quick barrel change—copied in the U.S. M73 tank machine gun. (*Fig* **59**)

185. Parachutists of First German Airborne Corps defending Cassino 1944. Firing at 1 200 rounds a minute the MG-42 was a very effective dual purpose machine gun. The Germans used it a lot on a tripod to produce fixed line fire. The British troops called it the 'Spandau'.

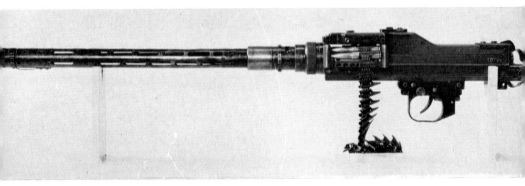

186. The Mauser MG-81 7.92mm aircraft gun. Single. The MG-34 action was applied to this aircraft gun. It had a powerful muzzle recoil intensifier producing 1 100 rounds a minute. In 1943 it was adapted for ground use.

187. Mauser MG-81 7.92mm aircraft machine gun. Twin. The high rate of fire of these two guns was very suitable for aircraft use. Its rifle calibre proved too small and it saw limited war service.

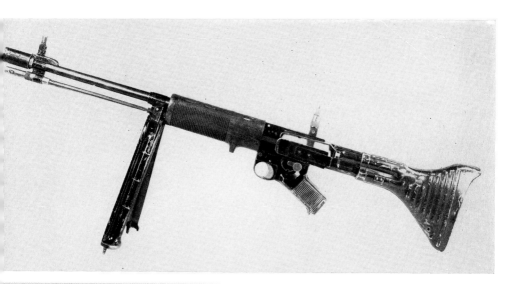

188. This shows the early metal butt and pistol grip version of the Krieghoff FG-42 7.92mm Parachutist's LMG. It was rushed into production when the parachutists on Crete, armed with the Schmeisser, were out-ranged by British and New Zealand rifle fire.

189. The later version of the sniper type FG-42. 7.92mm with laminated wood stock and pistol grip fitted with a telescopic sight. It was a remarkable weapon firing from a closed breech for rifle accuracy and open breech for LMG roles.

190. The Rheinmetall MG 42/59 was an MG-42 converted to NATO 7.62mm in 1959 when Germany joined NATO. German ammunition produces less peak pressure than U.K.—hence the warning on this gun that it has not had a British proof cartridge fired in it to produce a pressure 1.25 times normal pressure.

191. ▼ The final version of the Rheinmetall MG-3 7.62mm GPMG in service with the Federal Republic Armed Forces. It fires at either 1 200 or 600 rounds/minute changed by an internal bolt adjustment. The photo shows the barrel being changed which is one of the very good features of this gun.

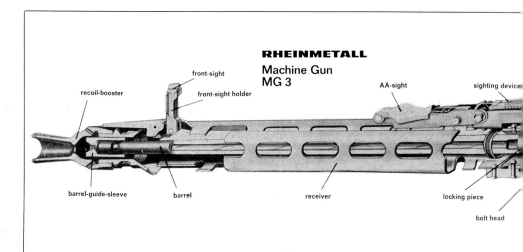

RHEINMETALL
Machine Gun
MG 3

front-sight
front-sight holder
recoil-booster
AA-sight
sighting device
barrel-guide-sleeve
barrel
receiver
locking piece
bolt head

192. A sectioned drawing of the Rheinmetall MG-3. The bolt action of this gun is described in the main text. The powerful steel buffer which is largely responsible for the high rate of fire is shown well, above.

193. In 1945 German Arms Technologists went to the Centro de Estudios Technicos de Materiales Especiales in Madrid and the resulting automatic rifle shown here was developed by Heckler & Koch, Oberndorf, into the standard German G3 rifle. This delayed blowback design was the forerunner of the machine gun which follows.

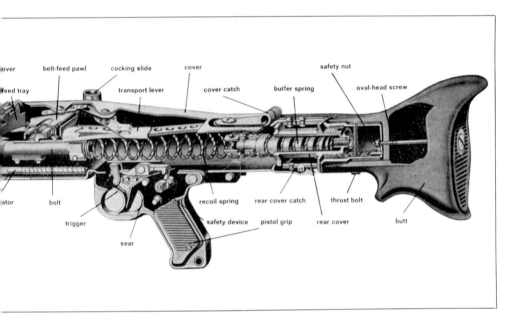

over   belt-feed pawl   cocking slide   cover   safety nut

feed tray   transport lever   cover catch   buffer spring   oval-head screw

ator   bolt   recoil spring   rear cover catch   thrust bolt

trigger   safety device   pistol grip   rear cover   butt

sear

194. Heckler and Koch HK13 .223 LMG. This can be drum fed or take a 40 round box magazine. It has been tested in this country and found to be very reliable under adverse conditions. It will produce a sustained rate of about 40 rounds a minute or short bursts at a higher rate.

Italian Machine Guns

195. Fiat Revelli model 1914 6.5mm. Note the unusual feed arrangement for a sustained fire machine gun. With the water jacket removed this became the aircraft machine gun model 1914 6.5mm.

196. Originally designed as an aircraft observer's gun, in 1917, the Villa Perosa LMG 9mm twin barrel blowback gun was used on motor cycle combinations and as a LMG in the Alpine campaign. It fired at 1000 rpm from each barrel. Each magazine held 20 rounds.

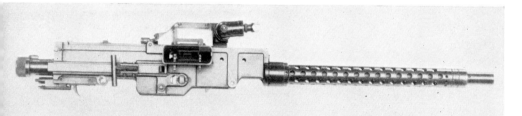

197. Breda model 1928 6.5mm. The 1924 model was improved somewhat and called the model 1928. Only 2 000 were made.

198. The Breda model 1930 6.5mm, standard LMG for the Italian Army in the North African desert. The lubricated cartridge and loose fitting barrel were not ideal for desert conditions.

199. Breda Safat model 1935 aircraft machine gun 7.7mm. With a rate of fire of 800 rounds a minute and weighing only 27 pounds this was the standard World War II Italian aircraft gun.

200. Breda machine gun model 1937 8mm. The standard Italian MMG, this gun replaced the empty cases in the strip—which hardly helped when reloading in action!

201. The Breda machine gun model 1938. 8mm, universally used as a tank machine gun.

202. Scotti 7.7mm machine guns. Both the aircraft machine gun (left) and the LMG worked on the principle of using gas to unlock and blowback to operate.

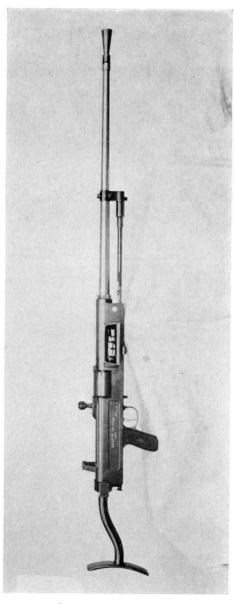

Japanese Machine Guns

203. The Type 3 (1914) was a direct copy of the Hotchkiss Model 1914 carried out by the Koishikawa Army Arsenal at Tokyo. General Nambu changed the ejector to a Lewis type but this was the only alteration.

204. This 1922 Japanese design by General Nambu, the Taishio 11 LMG 6.5mm, had a unique hopper feed which took 6 chargers each of five rounds of the type used in the 6.5mm Arisaka rifle. It was also used in tanks and with a larger hopper was called the Type 91 (1931).

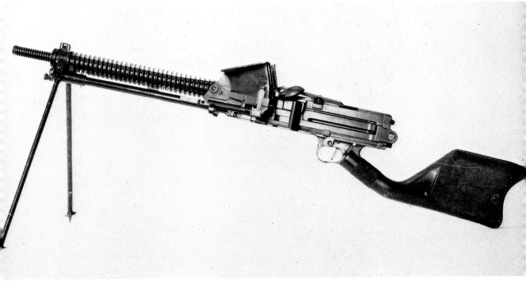

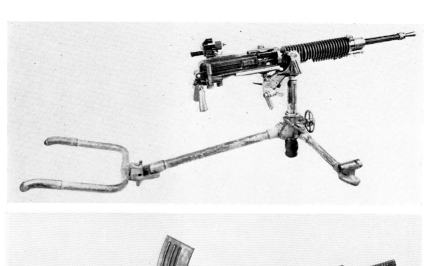

FACING PAGE

205. Type 92 MMG 7.7mm semi-rimless 1932. Nambu improved the Type 3, which was a Hotchkiss machine gun, and used the type 92 round. The type 99 round which was rimless could also be used. The gun was carried on its tripod by putting carrying bars through the tubes on the front legs whilst the third man carried the yoke. It weighed 122lb on the tripod.

206. Type 96 LMG 6.5mm 1936. This was based on the Czech Zb 26 gun with a Lewis type ejector. The cartridges were oiled by the magazine filler.

207. Type 99 LMG 7.7mm rimless 1939. The type 96 was improved to take the type 99 ammunition without lubrication. It had a vivid muzzle flash. Used very widely by the Japanese in World War II.

208. Type 100 and Type 1 7.92mm. Model 1, shown, has a shoulder harness. Model 100 has not. This was an aircraft machine gun of the Bren type with a 100 round magazine, weighing 36lbs and firing at 400–600rpm.

209. Machine gun 5M Cal .30. A prototype gun (left) designed by Dr. Masaya Kawamura and produced by Nittoku Metal Industry. It fired the .30–06 cartridge at 450–550rpm and was based on the Czech Zb design. There was a heavy barrel version (right) tripod mounted for sustained fire.

210. Machine gun 7M 7.62mm NATO. A prototype gun (top) also by Dr Masaya Kawamura. It could be either left or right hand feed and had a heavy barrel, tripod mounted, sustained fire version (below).

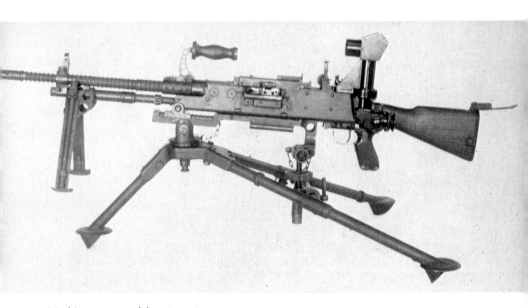

211. Machine gun model 1963 7.62mm NATO. The current GPMG in the Japanese armed forces. Designed by Kawamura it is the first native product adopted since World War II and replaces American Brownings.

Russian Machine Guns

212. Made in Denmark, the Madsen LMG was widely used in Europe. The Russians equipped cavalry with it.

213. Maxim model 1910 7.62mm on Sokolov carriage. This gun and mounting were used by the Russians in the two World Wars and by the Chinese in Korea. Note the tractor radiator cap on the water jacket.

214. The basic Maxim was lightened by Tokarev to give the Maxim-Tokarev 7.62mm. The weapon was successfully used in the Spanish Civil War.

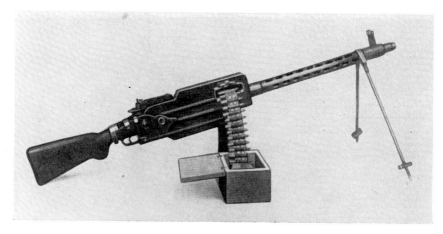

215. This Degtyarev LMG 7.62mm is the DP or Infantry gun. It was the main infantry section light gun throughout World War II. No one knows how many hundreds of thousands of these were made. They are still being used in Vietnam. The flat round drum is spring operated.

216. The Russians used the Degtyarev tank machine gun 7.62mm DT gun for ball mounts, turrets and free anti-aircraft fire. It went in one role or another into all their tanks in World War II.

217. The Goryunov M43 MMG 7.62mm, used in the Russian Army from its inception in 1943 to the early '60s. It is now standard Chinese equipment and is being employed by the North Vietnamese regular troops.

218. The Goryunov M43 in action. The Russians have equipped the Regular Armies of the Arab countries encircling Israel and also the guerrillas. An El Fatah anti-aircraft team is seen firing at an Israeli aircraft.

219. SGT in tank mounting. The M43 was modified by taking the cocking handle from between the spade grips and putting it on the right hand side of the body, fitting a finned barrel and a new cartridge head space adjuster. The Infantry version is the SGM, the tank—shown—the SGT.

220. RP-46, the company machine gun. This post-war gun is a DP with a heavy barrel and a detachable top cover plate for the magazine fitment. It has not been observed in use in any quantity.

221. RPD in action. Arab guerrillas in Southern Syria using the RPD, Degtyarev, belt fed LMG. The RPD fires the M43 7.62mm × 39 intermediate round. All the Russian weapons previously shown have taken the big 7.62mm × 54 rimmed round.

222. RPK 7.62mm × 39. This is the latest Russian light machine gun and it displaced the RPD. It has the 40 round box magazine shown or a 75 round drum magazine mounted below the gun at right angles to the barrel. Its maximum effective range is about 800 metres.

223. Russian soldiers firing the RPK. Notice the under hand grip of the left hand on the small of the butt.

224. The PK GPMG (7.62mm × 54R). The Russians have introduced this gun into the Infantry Battalion very recently. It may well supersede the SGM and SGT.

225. The PK firing. The Russians have abandoned their old wheeled carriage and now use a buffered tripod.

226. The DK 12.7mm HMG 1934. Very few of these were made but it had a much better finish than any previous Russian gun.

227. The Degtyarev at Stalingrad—1943. The original sprocket feed designed by Shpagin for this 12.7mm HMG lies under the circular casing over the breech. This gun was employed extensively on AA work.

FACING PAGE

228. The Degtyarev M1938/46. This 12.7mm HMG has a Degtyarev feed and a flat top cover plate. It is a very reliable hard hitting gun.

229. The Degtyarev M1938/46 on an armoured personnel carrier during an assault water crossing.

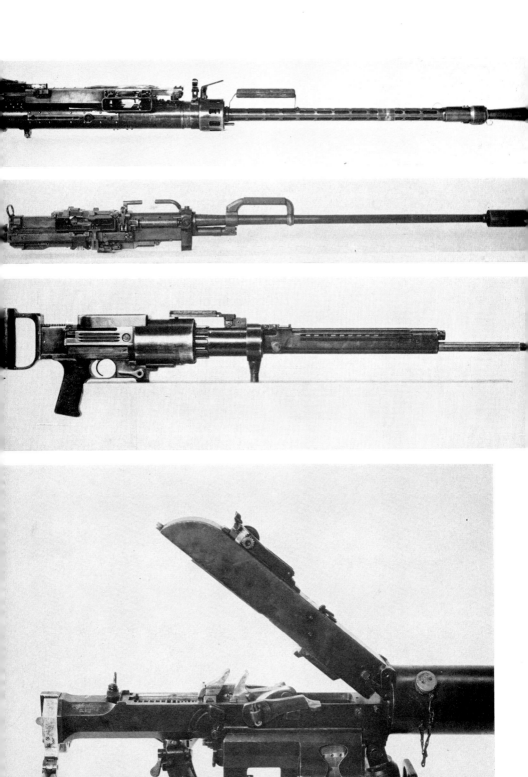

230. KPV 14.5mm tank machine gun. This was designed around the PTR anti-tank cartridge and it has a very high velocity. It has been used as an anti-aircraft gun but may be seen in Infantry Armoured Personnel Carriers.

231. Based on a German Krieghoff rising lock design, the future employment of this gun, the Zu 23mm cannon, is a matter of some interest. It may well appear in the APC to be used to destroy similar vehicles.

232. Skhas aircraft machine gun 7.62mm. This war-time machine gun had a very complicated feed cage and an unusual 2-stage ejection system. It fired a special round of its own.

Other Machine Guns

233. The Austrian Schwartsloze 8mm MMG, a delayed blowback machine gun developed in 1908 and used as late as 1945. The barrel length is very critical.

234. The Czech Vz 52; developed from the Zb pattern this gun fired either belt or magazine. It was a complex weapon, using the Czech M52 7.62mm intermediate cartridge accurately out to 800 metres.

235. The Czech 1959 GPMG. Although this gun was developed to fire the Russian 7.62mm × 54R cartridge, it can also be bought in NATO 7.62mm. It will produce indirect fire to 5 000 metres.

236. The Danish Madsen-Saetter 7.62mm GPMG. This gun was tested in the U.K. in 1958 but not adopted here.

237. The SIG MG 35. The Swiss Industrial Corporation at Neuhausen produced this prototype gas operated gun with two 50 round magazines.

238. This gas operated SIG MG 50 prototype for the Swiss Army was one of the earliest machine guns to fit an infra-red night sight.

239. The breech mechanism designed for the blowback operated Mauser MG 45 incorporating a two part roller delay device, is used in this gun, the SIG MG 710–3. It is very efficient and has the fastest barrel change of any GPMG yet produced.

255

240. The Swiss Oerlikon 35mm AA gun. This picture is included to show the complexity of the modern anti-aircraft gun, and this is probably the most highly developed gun yet produced—the muzzle velocity is measured as each round is fired and a correction made to the next round if there is any variation from the normal.